BERTRAND R

MODERN MASTERS

Already published

ALBERT CAMUS / Conor Cruise O'Brien
FRANTZ FANON / David Caute
HERBERT MARCUSE / Alasdair MacIntyre
CHE GUEVARA / Andrew Sinclair
CLAUDE LEVI-STRAUSS / Edmund Leach
LUDWIG WITTGENSTEIN / David Pears
GEORGE LUKÁCS / George Lichtheim
NOAM CHOMSKY / John Lyons
JAMES JOYCE / John Gross
MARSHALL MCLUHAN / Jonathan Miller
GEORGE ORWELL / Raymond Williams
SIGMUND FREUD / Richard Wollheim
WILLIAM BUTLER YEATS /
   Denis Donoghue
WILHELM REICH / Charles Rycroft
MOHANDAS GANDHI / George Woodcock
V. I. LENIN / Robert Conquest
NORMAN MAILER / Richard Poirier

MODERN MASTERS

EDITED BY frank kermode

bertrand russell

a. j. ayer

NEW YORK | THE VIKING PRESS

Published in 1972 in a hardbound
and paperbound edition by
The Viking Press, Inc.
625 Madison Avenue, New York, N.Y. 10022
SBN 670–15899–2 (hardbound)
670–01950–x (paperbound)
Library of Congress catalog card number: 76–181979
Printed in U.S.A.

To Charito and Alex Gonzalez

PREFACE

In this book I have attempted to give, in a relatively short compass, an account of the major incidents of Bertrand Russell's life, and an exposition of the whole range of his philosophy in a form that will be intelligible to those who are not experts in the subject. I have not avoided entering into technical questions, but I have used technical terms as sparingly as possible and when I have used them have given some explanation of their meaning. In dealing with the more technical aspects of Russell's philosophy, I have drawn very freely upon my book *Russell and Moore: The Analytical Heritage*, which was published in 1971 by Macmillan in England and by the Harvard University Press in the United States, and I have to thank these publishers for allowing me to do so. I apologize to those of my readers who have read the earlier book, but it seemed to me foolish to go to the labor of rewriting what I had already expressed as well and clearly as I could.

My thanks are again due to Mrs. Guida Crowley for typing the manuscript of this book and helping me to prepare it for the press.

A. J. AYER

10 Regents Park Terrace
London, N.W.1.
September 23, 1971

C O N T E N T S

Preface   ix

i / Russell's Life and Works   1

ii / Russell's Philosophy of Logic   29

     A The Motives for Logical Construction   29

     B The Reduction of Mathematics to Logic   35

     C The Theory of Types   42

     D The Theory of Descriptions   48

     E Russell's Theories of Belief and of Truth   59

iii / Russell's Theory of Knowledge   69

     A His Theories of Perception   69

     B On Self-Consciousness and Memory   86

     C His Theory of Induction   92

Contents | *xii*

iv / Russell's Conception of Reality   103
 A His Logical Atomism   103
 B Mind and Matter   112
v / Russell's Moral Philosophy   117
 A Ethics   117
 B Religion   130
 C Politics   138
 Short Bibliography   157
 Index   159

BERTRAND RUSSELL

Russell's Life and Works

i

Bertrand Russell was unique among the philosophers of this century in combining the study of the specialized problems of philosophy, not only with an interest in both the natural and the social sciences, but with an engagement in primary as well as higher education, and an active participation in politics. It was, indeed, mainly through his political activity and as a moral and social propagandist that he achieved the worldwide fame which he enjoyed at the end of his life, but it is to his philosophical work, and especially that which he accomplished in his youth and early middle age, that he will owe his place in history. Here too, his range was exceptionally wide. He himself, no doubt with good reason, attached the greatest value to the work which he did on mathematical logic; but we shall see that he also made an important contribution to the philosophy of logic in a wider sense, to the theory of knowledge, and to ontology, the question of what there really is. In all these aspects, his work has had a very great influence upon his contemporaries, from the beginning of this century up to the present day. Indeed, with the possible exception of his pupil Ludwig Wittgenstein, there is no philosopher of our time who has made such a large difference not only to the treatment of particular philosophical problems but to the way in which the whole subject is pursued.

Russell was born on May 18, 1872, almost exactly a year before the death of his lay godfather, John Stuart Mill. His father, Viscount Amberley, was the eldest son of the first Earl Russell, the famous Liberal statesman who, as Lord John Russell, introduced the first Reform Bill in 1832 and was twice Prime Minister, from 1846 to 1852 and from 1865 to 1866. His mother, who also belonged to the Whig aristocracy, was the daughter of a less prominent Liberal politician, the second Lord Stanley of Alderley. Bertrand Arthur William Russell was their second son and third child. Their lives and characters are sympathetically depicted in the two volumes of *The Amberley Papers* which Russell edited in collaboration with Patricia Russell, his third wife, and published in 1937.

Russell's mother and sister died of diphtheria in 1874, and his father, who never recovered from this loss, survived them by less than two years. He had appointed two freethinkers as guardians of his sons but his parents contrived to have this provision nullified, with the result that Bertrand Russell and his brother Frank, who was nearly seven years his senior, went to live with their grandparents at Pembroke Lodge, a grace-and-favor house in Richmond Park which Queen Victoria had given to Lord and Lady Russell for their lifetime. In the first and most fascinating of the three volumes of autobiography which Russell published in the years 1966–1969 he speaks of his arrival at Pembroke Lodge at the age of three as his earliest vivid recollection. His grandfather, who was then eighty-three years of age, lived only three years longer, but his grandmother, who was twenty-three years younger than her husband and lived until 1898, was the dominant influence on him throughout his childhood and adolescence. A daughter of the second Earl of Minto, she came from a family of staunch Presbyterians and held very strong moral and religious convictions. In politics she was more radical than her husband, and her influence over him was resented by his colleagues, who spoke of her as "Deadly Night-shade." Bertrand Russell himself came to reject many of her principles, though not her radicalism, but he inherited her moral fervor: and the text which she inscribed on the flyleaf of the Bible which she gave him, "Thou shalt not follow a multitude to do evil," was one to which he courageously adhered at all times in his life.

As he recalls it in his autobiography, Russell's childhood was solitary but not unhappy. Unlike his brother, he was not sent away to school, but was educated by governesses and tutors. In adolescence, he began to suffer from loneliness, and he was made unhappy by his sense of an intellectual estrangement from his grandmother which was sharpened by his rejection of her religious beliefs. His own interest in science had been aroused by one of his uncles at an early age, but the moment of his greatest intellectual awakening was his discovery of the geometry of Euclid, to which he was introduced by his brother at the age of eleven. He mastered the theorems very quickly but objected to having to take the axioms on trust. He consented to do so only when his brother assured him that they could make no progress otherwise. It was, however, a concession to which he was never really reconciled, as his philosophy was later to show.

After spending eighteen months at an Army crammer's, where he was shocked by the coarse philistinism of most of his companions, Russell succeeded in obtaining a minor scholarship in mathematics at Trinity College, Cambridge. He went up to Cambridge in October 1890, at the age of eighteen, and from then on, as he put it, "everything went well with me."[1] He had been examined for the scholarship by A. N. Whitehead, with whom he was afterward to collaborate on *Principia Mathematica*, and Whitehead had told people to look out for him. He quickly made a circle of friends which included the philosopher J. E. McTaggart, then already a lecturer at Cambridge, and was later to include the philosopher G. E. Moore, and like them, he was elected a member of the exclusive society of The Apostles. He began by reading mathematics and was placed seventh Wrangler in the Mathematical Tripos of 1893, but his interest was already turning toward philosophy, and he stayed for a fourth year in order to read for the second part of the Moral Science Tripos. Having obtained a First with distinction, he set about working for a Fellowship.

By that time he was engaged to be married. He had met Alys Pearsall Smith in 1889, when he was barely seventeen, and had fallen instantly in love with her, though it was not until four years later that she began to take him seriously. She was five years older than he and came from a family of American Quakers: the writer Logan Pearsall Smith was her brother. Russell's family disapproved of the engagement, partly on social grounds, and tried to discourage him by telling him that the insanity in his family made it unsafe for him to have children: his uncle William was mad and his maiden Aunt Agatha, at the time of her own engagement, had

[1] *The Autobiography of Bertrand Russell*, I, 56.

suffered from insane delusions, so that the engagement had to be broken. When this did not deter him, they separated him from Alys by arranging for him to become an honorary attaché at the British Embassy in Paris. By his own account, his work there chiefly consisted in trying to persuade the French Government that lobsters were not fish. Tiring quickly of such diplomacy, and having a legacy from his father which made him financially independent, he returned to England after a few months, still determined upon marriage. The marriage took place in December 1894 and at the beginning turned out very happily.

In the following year Russell obtained his Fellowship at Trinity with a dissertation on the foundations of geometry. By the terms of the Fellowship, which he held until 1901, he was not required to teach or even to reside in Cambridge, and he went with his wife to Berlin to study politics and economics. Many years later he wrote of a spring morning when, walking in the Tiergarten, he formed the plan of writing two series of books: one "on the philosophy of the sciences, growing gradually more concrete as I passed from mathematics to biology" and the other "on social and political questions, growing gradually more abstract."[2] Being still under the influence of the Hegelianism which he had learned from McTaggart, he hoped that this would culminate in a Hegelian synthesis, "an encyclopaedic work dealing equally with theory and practice."[3] The earliest fruits of this project were the publication in 1896 of a work on *German Social Democracy*, the first of the seventy-one books and pamphlets that Russell was eventually to publish, and the appearance a year later of

[2] "My Mental Development," in P. A. Schilpp, ed., *The Philosophy of Bertrand Russell* (1944), p. 11.
[3] *Ibid.*

An Essay on the Foundations of Geometry, on the basis of his fellowship thesis. This was followed in 1900 by *A Critical Exposition of the Philosophy of Leibniz,* a book arising out of a course of lectures which, substituting for McTaggart, he had given at Cambridge in 1899. It mainly consisted in an attempt to derive Leibniz's metaphysics from his logic and in particular from his mistaken assumption that all propositions are of the subject-predicate form. By this time Russell had forsaken Hegel, chiefly through the persuasion of his friend G. E. Moore, but both in his book on Leibniz and still more in the earlier essay on the foundations of geometry he shows himself to have been strongly influenced by Kant, a philosopher for whom he later came to have little respect.

Russell's work on the philosophy of mathematics took a new and decisive turn in July 1900 when he went to an International Congress of Philosophy in Paris and there met the Italian logician Giuseppe Peano. Peano had developed his own system of mathematical logic, and Russell found in his notation "an instrument of logical analysis such as I had been seeking for years."[4] In fact, Peano's notation is rather cumbersome, and Russell himself was greatly to improve upon it, but it opened his eyes to the technical possibility of carrying out a reduction of mathematics to logic. Russell spent two months in mastering and extending Peano's methods and then turned with such ardor to the task of analyzing the fundamental notions of mathematics that he completed the first draft of his five-hundred-page book on *The Principles of Mathematics* by the end of the year. He took more than a year longer to revise it, and the book was not published until 1903. It remains a landmark in the history of the subject. We shall see that

[4] *The Autobiography of Bertrand Russell,* I, 144.

it contains a vein of Platonic Realism which Russell was later to reject, but, as he said in the introduction to the second edition, which appeared in 1937, its "fundamental thesis . . . that mathematics and logic are identical, is one which I have never since seen any reason to modify."[5]

To sustain this thesis, Russell needed to refashion logic, and for this he enlisted the cooperation of his old tutor, Whitehead. Together they set about constructing the new system of logic which is embodied in their *Principia Mathematica*, of which the first volume appeared in 1910, the second in 1912, and the third in 1913. At first everything went smoothly, but at a quite early stage, even before the publication of Russell's *The Principles of Mathematics*, they encountered difficulties which they were unable to resolve, until Russell in 1906 discovered his Theory of Types.[6] What chiefly remained after that was the mechanical labor of writing out the theorems. Since Whitehead was fully occupied with teaching, this devolved almost entirely upon Russell, who relates that from 1907 to 1910 he worked at it for about eight months in each year from ten to twelve hours a day.[7] When the book was completed, the syndics of the Cambridge University Press estimated that its publication would involve them in a loss of £600 of which they were not willing to bear more than half. The Royal Society, of which Russell and Whitehead were both Fellows, Russell having been elected in 1908, agreed to contribute £200, but the authors had to find the remaining £100. Thus, their financial reward for this masterpiece, which had cost them ten years' work, was minus £50 apiece.

---

[5] *The Principles of Mathematics*, p. v.
[6] See below, pp. 42–47.
[7] *The Autobiography of Bertrand Russell*, I, 152.

During this period the Russells and the Whiteheads frequently shared a house. Mrs. Whitehead was an invalid, suffering from heart trouble, and Russell describes an occasion, in the year 1901, when finding her isolated in her pain he had a sudden revelation of "the loneliness of the human soul." He reflected that "nothing can penetrate it except the highest intensity of the sort of love that religious teachers have preached; whatever does not spring from this motive is harmful, or at best useless; it follows that war is wrong, that a public school education is abominable, that the use of force is to be deprecated, and that in human relations one should penetrate to the core of loneliness in each person and speak to that."[8] Russell was never a theist or, as we shall see, a friend to organized religion, but he was a man of religious temper. In his youth, his attitude to mathematics was almost mystical,[9] he was always sensitive to nature and to romantic poetry, and his desire that human existence should have a meaning was reflected in the emotional stresses of his private life and in the passion which he brought to politics. At the same time, this mystical strain was balanced by a strong sense of irony, and by a skeptical and analytical intelligence; and it makes little showing in his philosophy.

During the years that he was working on *Principia Mathematica*, Russell did not allow his interest in politics to lapse. He was a friend of the leading Fabians, including Bernard Shaw and H. G. Wells and especially Beatrice and Sidney Webb, and under the Webbs' influence he had become an imperialist and a supporter of the Boer war. After the revelation which he underwent in 1901, he changed sides on this question and then

[8] *Ibid.*, p. 146.
[9] See, for example, his essay on "The Study of Mathematics" written in 1902 and reprinted in *Philosophical Essays* (1910) and *Mysticism and Logic* (1917).

became a pacifist. In the early years of the century he campaigned for Free Trade, and when this policy triumphed with the Liberal victory in the General Election of 1906, he took up the cause of women's suffrage. In the face of much ridicule and some violence, he stood unsuccessfully for Parliament at a by-election in Wimbledon in 1907 as a candidate for the National Union of Women's Suffrage Societies. After completing *Principia Mathematica* he thought more seriously of a political career and sought to have himself adopted as the Liberal candidate for Bedford. But the members of the local Liberal Association, who had at first received him enthusiastically, declined to select him when he confessed to being an agnostic and admitted that this fact would probably become known to the electors.

Russell believed, I do not know with how much justification, that his agnosticism also at this time cost him a Fellowship at Trinity.[10] By then he welcomed paid employment as he had diminished his capital in settling Whitehead's debts. Mrs. Whitehead knew of this but Whitehead himself did not. In fact Trinity did come to his support by making him, not indeed a Fellow, but a Lecturer. The appointment was made in 1910 for an initial period of five years. It carried the same salary as if it had been a Fellowship but did not give him any voice in the government of the College or afford him the same security of tenure. This fact was to become important a few years later.

The first decade of the century was a period not only of intellectual strain for Russell but also of emotional unhappiness. Early in 1902, when he was living with the Whiteheads at Grantchester, he went out bicycling one afternoon, and suddenly realized that he no longer loved Alys. He could not and indeed did not try to con-

[10] See *Sceptical Essays*, p. 150.

ceal this from her and since she continued to demonstrate a love for him to which he could not respond, while neither of them sought consolation with anybody else, their life together became difficult to bear. This went on for nine years until Russell fell in love with Lady Ottoline Morrell, the famous hostess of Garsington, and the wife of a Liberal politician for whom Russell had been canvassing. When he confessed this to Alys, she threatened to divorce him and cite Lady Ottoline. But Lady Ottoline did not wish to leave her husband or to incur a scandal, and Russell prevented Alys from taking action by threatening to commit suicide. He then went away and did not see Alys again until 1950, when they met as friends. It is clear from her letters that she loved him all her life.

Though Russell had been concentrating on mathematical logic since he began work on *The Principles of Mathematics*, he had not entirely neglected other aspects of philosophy. His *Philosophical Essays*, which came out in 1910, contained a paper on ethics and some effective criticism of both pragmatist and idealist theories of truth, and his article "On Denotation," which indeed arose out of his logical studies and was published in *Mind* in 1905, laid the foundations of his famous Theory of Descriptions.[11] After completing *Principia Mathematica* he branched out further. The article in which he first made his important distinction between knowledge by acquaintance and knowledge by description[12] was published in 1911; his presidential address to the Aristotelian Society in the same year was concerned with the relation of particulars and universals,[13] and in 1912 he published in The Home University Library a little

[11] See below, pp. 48–58.
[12] See below, pp. 30–35.
[13] See below, pp. 103–112.

book on *The Problems of Philosophy*, which is probably still the best introduction to the subject that exists in English. In the following year he published among other things an important article, "On the Notion of Cause," and in the spring of 1914 he delivered the Lowell Lectures in Boston and published them under the title of *Our Knowledge of the External World as a Field for Scientific Method in Philosophy*. The position taken in this book, as we shall see, is that of a radical empiricism. It places Russell in the line of succession to Locke, Berkeley, Hume, and John Stuart Mill.

While he was lecturing at Boston Russell was made a temporary Professor at Harvard and there had T. S. Eliot as one of his graduate students. He is the hero of Eliot's poem "Mr. Apollinax," represented at a party where "his laughter tinkled among the teacups" and "his dry and passionate talk devoured the afternoon." He subsequently became a close friend of Eliot's and of Eliot's first wife's, but never succeeded in converting him to his philosophy.

By this time Russell's affair with Lady Ottoline Morrell was on the wane, and on this visit to the United States he again fell in love, with a girl who followed him to England on the understanding that she would live with him and that they would get married if Alys would give him a divorce. This plan was frustrated because Russell's love for her did not withstand the emotional shock to him of the outbreak of the First World War. Russell was not devoid of patriotism; indeed, he said in his autobiography that "love of England is very nearly the strongest emotion that I possess": [14] neither was he an absolute pacifist; in the Second World War he thought that the evils of Nazism warranted armed resistance. It was just that in 1914, and increasingly as the

[14] *The Autobiography of Bertrand Russell*, II, 7.

war progressed, he could see no principle at stake, or any probability of a better outcome, which would justify the suffering and loss of life. He was appalled by the enthusiasm with which our entry into the war was generally greeted and by the support which it found among many of his friends, including such men as Whitehead and Gilbert Murray. Being unable to achieve the detachment of his friend the philosopher Santayana, who reasoned that the young men who were being killed in the war would anyhow die sooner or later, and would be good for nothing while they lived, he devoted himself to writing against the war, making speeches at pacifist meetings, and taking an active part in such movements as the Union of Democratic Control and the No Conscription Fellowship. He did not believe that these activities could have much effect but thought it his duty to do whatever he could.

This duty extended to the attempt to work out a political theory which would supply the framework of a better order of society. The two books which resulted were *Principles of Social Reconstruction*, which was published in 1916, and *Roads to Freedom*, which came out two years later. In composing the lectures on which the first of these books was based, Russell had the advice of D. H. Lawrence. He had got to know Lawrence through Lady Ottoline, of whom Lawrence drew a malicious portrait as Hermione Roddice in his novel *Women in Love*. Lawrence's attitude to Russell was a mixture of friendship and hostility, with the hostility becoming predominant. He wrote asking Russell to make him his heir but in the same letter attacked him for being a savant, bidding him to "become a creature instead of a mechanical instrument,"[15] and he suggested that Russell's pacifism was a mask for his "lust to jab

[15] Quoted in Russell's *Portraits from Memory*, p. 109.

and strike." For a short while Russell believed this and was driven to thoughts of suicide, but then he threw off Lawrence's spell and saw his fascist politics and his cult of unreason for the evils that they were.

A better and braver friend was Clifford Allen, afterward Lord Allen of Hurtwood, the chairman of the No Conscription Fellowship, who was repeatedly court-martialed and kept in prison for refusing to obey military orders. It was at one of these trials in 1916 that Russell met Lady Constance Malleson, wife of the actor Miles Malleson and herself a well-known actress under the name of Colette O'Niel. They soon became lovers, and Russell found in her beauty and youth and courage, and in her love for him, a refuge from "the world of hate"[16] by which he was surrounded.

His enmity to this world was reciprocated by it. In April 1916 the No Conscription Fellowship had issued a leaflet in protest against a sentence of two years' hard labor which had been passed upon a conscientious objector. When some men were also sentenced to hard labor for distributing the leaflet, Russell wrote a letter to *The Times*, saying that he was the author of the leaflet and that if anyone was to be prosecuted for it, he was primarily responsible. As a result, he was brought to trial before the Lord Mayor of London on a charge of making "statements likely to prejudice the recruiting and discipline of His Majesty's forces." In fact the paragraph in the leaflet on which the prosecution chiefly relied, where the reader was asked whether he would join the persecutors or stand for those who were defending conscience, was not written by Russell, but he took responsibility for it. He was found guilty and sentenced to a fine of £100 with £10 costs or the alternative of 61 days' imprisonment. Russell refused to pay the fine,

[16] *The Autobiography of Bertrand Russell*, II, 26.

but when the authorities distrained on his effects, his friends raised the money and offered it for the first of his books to be put up for auction.

The most serious consequence to Russell of this affair was that he was dismissed from his position at Trinity. In February 1915 the Council of the College had declared its willingness to appoint him to a Fellowship as soon as his Lectureship expired, but when he applied for two terms' leave of absence in order to continue his political work, the Council decided to renew his Lectureship for a further five years instead. When its members heard of his conviction, they voted unanimously to remove him from the Lectureship. As the executive body of the College, they had the power to do this, but the attitude of the eleven men concerned, who were mostly elderly and politically out of sympathy with Russell, was at variance with that of the majority of the Fellows, including those who were serving in the war. Twenty-two of them immediately signed a letter of protest, and in 1919, a year after the end of the war, a memorial demanding Russell's reinstatement, which was signed by twenty-eight Fellows and supported by five others, was agreed to by the Council. Russell accepted the appointment, but applied for leave of absence for the year 1920–1921, and in 1921, when he was due to resume his lectures, he resigned because he feared that the circumstances of his second marriage might bring scandal on the College and embarrass his friends.[17]

In the meantime Russell continued his conflict with authority. When Trinity dismissed him he was offered a Professorship at Harvard, but the British Government refused him a passport. Two years later they took

[17] The foregoing account is based on G. H. Hardy's *Bertrand Russell and Trinity*. Professor Hardy was himself one of Russell's most active supporters in Trinity.

stronger action. In May 1918 he wrote an article for a weekly paper, in which, in the course of depicting the bad consequences which would result from refusing the German overtures for peace, he wrote, "the American Garrison which will by that time be occupying England and France, whether or not they will prove efficient against the Germans, will no doubt be capable of intimidating strikers, an occupation to which the American Army is accustomed when at home."[18] For this alleged libel on an ally, he was sent to prison for six months. Thanks to the intervention of Mr. Balfour, he served the sentence under conditions which allowed him the free use of books and writing materials, and he took advantage of this opportunity to write his *Introduction to Mathematical Philosophy*, in which he gives a lucid and simple account of the main ideas of *Principia Mathematica*, and to begin work on *The Analysis of Mind*.

The decision to return to philosophy had been taken by Russell even before he wrote the article which landed him in prison. Early in 1918 he had given in London a course of eight lectures entitled *The Philosophy of Logical Atomism*. They were published then in *The Monist*, but did not appear in book form until 1956, when they were included in a collection of Russell's essays entitled *Logic and Knowledge*. As Russell admitted in the preface to the lectures which he wrote for *The Monist*, they owed a great deal to conversations which he had had with Ludwig Wittgenstein before the war. Wittgenstein had come to Cambridge in 1912 to learn the philosophy of mathematics from Russell and had very soon impressed Russell with his genius. When the war broke out, Wittgenstein became an officer in the Austrian army and was captured by the Italians

[18] *The Autobiography of Bertrand Russell*, II, 80.

some time after the Armistice. In his acknowledgment in *The Monist* Russell said that he did not know whether Wittgenstein was alive or dead, but in February 1919 Wittgenstein wrote to him from his Italian prison camp to say that he had a manuscript which he would like Russell to read and that when he ceased to be a prisoner of war he would like them to meet and discuss it. This was the manuscript of Wittgenstein's famous *Tractatus Logico-Philosophicus*. One obstacle to their meeting was that Wittgenstein, believing it wrong for a philosopher to have money, had given away his considerable fortune and was too proud to let Russell pay his fare. This difficulty was resolved by Russell's buying some furniture which Wittgenstein had left in Cambridge, and they met in The Hague at Christmas 1919. The result was that Russell arranged for the publication of the *Tractatus* and wrote an introduction to the English edition. After that they diverged philosophically. Wittgenstein coupled Russell with H. G. Wells as men who had run out of problems, and Russell, though he retained great affection for Wittgenstein, could see little merit in his later work.

In this visit to The Hague, Russell was accompanied by Dora Black, whom he had first met in 1916 when she was a student at Girton. Meeting her again in 1919 he was torn between her and Colette, but the fact that she wanted to have children made her the more attractive to him. They were, however, at odds politically because of their different attitudes to Soviet Russia, which they visited independently in 1920. Dora Black was favorably impressed by what she was shown there, but Russell, as he wrote to Lady Ottoline, though thinking it "the right government for Russia at this moment," saw the regime more percipiently as "a close tyrannical bureaucracy, with a spy system more elaborate and terrible than the Tsars'," ruling "a nation of artists" which it aimed to make "as industrial and as Yankee as possible."[19] He recorded his opinions in a book called *The Theory and Practice of Bolshevism*, which was published in the same year, and never relaxed his opposition to the Soviets' denial of liberty.

After returning from Russia Russell almost immediately left for China, where he had been invited to lecture for a year. He took Dora with him, intending to marry her as soon as the divorce proceedings which he had persuaded Alys to bring against him were completed. Russell was as enchanted with China as he had been disenchanted with Russia and was especially captivated by Peking, which seemed to me also, when I visited it in 1954, to be the most beautiful city in the world. Toward the end of his stay in China he became seriously ill with bronchitis, and very nearly died. Some Japanese journalists, who had been refused an interview, reported that he *had* died, which gave him the pleasure of reading his own obituary notices. One of them, in a missionary journal, consisted of the one sentence "Missionaries may be pardoned for breathing a sigh of relief at the news of Mr Bertrand Russell's death."

Having disappointed the missionaries, Russell returned to England in September 1921, and married Dora Black. Their first child was born soon afterward and named John Conrad, in part after the novelist Joseph Conrad, for whom Russell had a great admiration and affection, which Conrad reciprocated. A daughter, Kate, was born two years later. Since landlords refused to have him as a tenant, on moral and political grounds, Russell bought a house in Chelsea, where he stood unsuccessfully as a Labour candidate for Parliament in 1922 and again in 1923. For the sake of the children he also bought a house in Cornwall where he

---

[19] *The Autobiography of Bertrand Russell*, II, 122.

Which Way to Peace? in 1936, besides a short book on *Religion and Science* in 1935 and a lecture on *Determinism and Physics* in 1936. In *Which Way to Peace?* he still maintained a pacifist position but became increasingly dissatisfied with it as the Second World War approached.

The best of these books, in my view, is *Freedom and Organization 1814–1914*, in which Russell most effectively displays his gift for writing political history. In doing the research for this book he was assisted by Patricia, more commonly known as Peter, Spence, a young woman who had at one time taught at his school. In 1936 he married her, and their son, Conrad, was born in the following year.

Having published a book on *Power* in 1938, Russell again turned to philosophy. He gave a course of lectures at the London School of Economics and another at Oxford, where he held discussions with the younger philosophers, of whom I was one. He seemed to me then and later to have the great quality, which Moore and Einstein also had, of being able to talk to younger and less gifted people as though he could learn something from them.

In the autumn of 1938 Russell went with his family to America to take up an appointment as Visiting Professor at the University of Chicago. This was followed by a similar appointment at the University of California, and in 1940 he was invited by the Board of Higher Education of New York City to become a professor at their City College. But no sooner had he accepted this offer, and resigned from his post in California, than an outcry was raised against his appointment. It was started by an Episcopalian bishop and continued mainly by the Catholic hierarchy. The grounds of their objection to Russell were his agnosticism and his alleged advocacy and practice of sexual immorality. When the Board of

Higher Education stood firm, a Mrs. Kay of Brooklyn was induced to bring an action against the city to have Russell's appointment voided because of the harm which his teaching might do to her daughter. The fact that he had been invited to teach logic at a liberal arts college to which at that time women were not admissible was not considered relevant. Her lawyer, a Mr. Goldstein, drew heavily upon his imagination, describing Russell's works in his brief as "lecherous libidinous, lustful, venerous, erotomaniac, aphrodisiac, irreverent, narrow-minded, untruthful, and bereft of moral-fibre."[21] On the strength of Russell's sensible remark, in his book on *Education*, that "a child should, from the first, be allowed to see his parents and brothers and sisters without their clothes whenever it so happens naturally,"[22] he accused him of conducting a nudist colony, and he added, without any evidence at all, that Russell went in for salacious poetry and approved of homosexuality. Russell was not able to answer these charges in court since he was not allowed to become a party to the suit. The case was tried before a Roman Catholic judge called McGeehan, who found for the plaintiff mainly on the ground that Russell's teaching would encourage his pupils to commit criminal offenses. The Board of Higher Education was prevented from appealing on a legal technicality, and an appeal would anyhow have been of little use, as in the next city budget Mayor La Guardia prudently removed the appropriation for Russell's lectureship.

As a result of this affair, Russell was almost completely deprived of the means of earning a living in the

---

[21] *The Autobiography of Bertrand Russell*, II, 219. For a full account of the affair see also the appendix by Paul Edwards to the 1950 edition of Russell's *Why I am not a Christian*.
[22] *On Education: Especially in Early Childhood*, p. 170.

United States. Although many academic persons had spoken up in his defense, they could not persuade their universities to employ him. The lecture tour which he had planned had to be canceled, and no newspaper or magazine would print his articles. Happily, Harvard University, which had already invited him to give the William James Lectures, had the courage and decency to maintain its invitation. The lectures were published in the same year under the title of *An Inquiry into Meaning and Truth*. Though it leaves some loose ends, the book contains many interesting ideas and I rank it high among Russell's philosophical works.

Having completed his semester at Harvard, Russell was rescued from his predicament by Dr. Barnes, a Philadelphia millionaire who owned a magnificent collection of modern pictures, which he seldom allowed anyone to see, and maintained a private Foundation, mainly for the instruction of art historians. He invited Russell to lecture at the Foundation and gave him a five-year contract, which he broke after less than two years on the ground that the lectures, which were a preview of the greater part of Russell's *History of Western Philosophy*, were insufficiently prepared. On this occasion, Russell was more fortunate in his judge: he brought an action for wrongful dismissal against Barnes and was awarded damages. In the meantime he had been invited by Trinity to return as a Fellow. It was some time before the British Embassy could be persuaded to arrange for his and his family's passage home, in spite of his argument that he wished to perform his duties in the House of Lords, but an invitation from Professor Paul Weiss at Bryn Mawr College broke the embargo on his lecturing, and he obtained a substantial advance on the *History of Western Philosophy*, which turned out to be the most financially successful of all his books; so much so as to relieve him thenceforward of financial anxiety. At Bryn Mawr Russell completed the intellectual autobiography which he wrote for *The Philosophy of Bertrand Russell* in the series of The Library of Living Philosophers. This book, which was published in 1944, contains an interesting article on Russell's logic by Gödel and a moving appreciation of his work by Einstein, but the level of the contributions to it is more than usually uneven and Russell's reply to his critics is rather perfunctory.

Russell entered into his Fellowship at Trinity in October 1944 and gave lectures in Cambridge in that and the two ensuing academic years. His Fellowship was prolonged until 1949 and then changed to a Fellowship under another category which gave him tenure for life without any duties. *A History of Western Philosophy* was published in 1945 and was followed in 1948 by *Human Knowledge: Its Scope and Limits*, the last of Russell's major philosophical works. Russell was chagrined by the comparative lack of attention which professional philosophers paid to this book, and attributed it to the contemporary vogue for a narrow form of linguistic philosophy of which he disapproved. For the most part, the ideas which the book contains had already been set out in *An Inquiry into Meaning and Truth*, but it is of interest in that it contains Russell's first full-scale attempt to tackle the problem of induction.

After Trinity had welcomed him back, the British authorities also decided that Russell had become respectable, and indeed that his hostility to Communism could be turned to their advantage. In 1948 he was sent to lecture in Berlin, where to his great amusement he was temporarily made a member of the armed forces, and in November of the same year he went on a similar mission to Norway. On this occasion he was saved from death by his strong addiction to smoking, admittedly a pipe and not cigarettes, since the airplane which was taking him from Oslo to Trondheim crashed in Trondheim harbor and all the passengers in its non-smoking compartment were killed. Russell had to swim a short distance before he was picked up by a boat but was none the worse for the adventure, even though the water was icy cold. Though he looked very frail, he had a very strong constitution and except for an attack of pneumonia in 1953 which nearly killed him, and another severe illness ten years later, he enjoyed remarkably good health till the end of his life. In his later years he was afflicted with deafness and he also had difficulty in swallowing, which meant that he had to live upon soft foods, but he continued to enjoy smoking and drinking, especially whisky and champagne. I last saw him on his ninety-fifth birthday and found him physically active and intelligently alert. The rumor which was put about by his political adversaries that he became senile is quite without foundation.

Continuing in official favor, Russell was awarded the Order of Merit, eliciting from King George VI the comment that he was "a queer-looking man," and in the same year, 1949, was made an Honorary Fellow of the British Academy and invited by the BBC to give the first series of Reith Lectures, which he published under the title of *Authority and the Individual*. In 1950 he toured Australia and the United States, and then went to Stockholm to receive the Nobel Prize for literature. The speech which he made on this occasion is included in his book *Human Society in Ethics and Politics*, which came out in 1954. Among the other books which he published in the 1950s were the charming *Portraits from Memory*, consisting mainly of character sketches of some of the famous people that he had known, and *My Philosophical Development*, a combination of intellectual autobiography, replies to his critics, and statements of his current views. He also brought out two volumes of short stories, entitled *Satan in the Suburbs* and *Nightmares of Eminent Persons*. They are mainly fables, very much in the manner of Voltaire.

Russell's marriage to Patricia Spence broke up in 1949, and in 1952 he married Edith Finch, an American lady whom he had known for many years. This marriage was very happy and brought Russell a peace of mind which he had not previously known. At first they shared a house in Richmond with Russell's eldest son and his family, but in 1955 they rented a house at Penrhyn-deudraeth in North Wales, where, with occasional excursions, mainly on political business, Russell lived for the remainder of his life.

From that time onward, Russell was increasingly absorbed in politics. He was chiefly moved to action by his belief in the probability of a third world war, in which he feared that the use of atomic weapons would bring about the destruction of the greater part of the human race. There had been a period in the late 1940s when he had argued that the United States should coerce Russia by threatening to use the atom-bomb, but by the middle 1950s he had come to the conclusion that the only hope for peace lay in the renunciation of atomic weapons, as a prelude to general disarmament, and he thought it the British Government's duty to set the example. He held this opinion so strongly that he hardly admitted the possibility of honest disagreement, and he too readily accused his political adversaries of simple wickedness. His views are set out in his book *Common Sense and Nuclear Warfare*, which was published in 1959, and its sequel *Has Man a Future?*, which was published in 1961. His own long-term political solution was the establishment of a world government, for which he campaigned actively in the 1950s. In 1955 he induced a number of leading scientists, including Einstein and Joliot-Curie, to sign a manifesto in favor of cooperation for peace and inaugurated a series of annual conferences to this end. In 1958 he became President of the Campaign for Nuclear Disarmament, resigning two years later to head the Committee of 100 in its campaign of civil disobedience. In February 1961 he presided at the mass sit-down which it organized in Whitehall, and after another mass meeting in August, he and his wife were arrested and charged with incitement to civil disobedience. They were sentenced to two months' imprisonment but on the production of medical evidence that this would be dangerous to their health, the sentence was commuted to a week's detention in the prison hospital.

Thereafter Russell's activities broadened out. He corresponded with heads of states and intervened both in the Cuban crisis of 1962 and in the Sino-Indian border dispute. He took up the cause of the Jews in Russia, the Arabs in Israel, and political prisoners in East Germany and Greece. Rejecting the official account of President Kennedy's assassination, he became President of the British Who Killed Kennedy? Committee. In 1964 he established the Bertrand Russell Peace Foundation and to raise funds for it later sold his archives to McMasters University in Ontario. By now he had come to think that the action of the United States Government represented the greatest danger to world peace, and the last book which he published, apart from his autobiography, was entitled *War Crimes in Vietnam*. This came out in 1967, shortly after he had set up an International War Crimes Tribunal, of which Jean-Paul Sartre was the most prominent member, which arraigned President Johnson. The proceedings of this tribunal were ill received at the time, but the evidence which has since come to light has very largely vindicated them.

In his book on *Human Society in Ethics and Politics*

Russell said that in the ethical sphere he agreed with Hume's dictum that "Reason is and ought to be the slave of the passions." At times he may have followed this principle too literally, but whatever view one takes of his political position, one's admiration must be commanded by the moral fervor, the persistent concern for humanity, the amazing intellectual and physical energy which drove him on. He died on February 2, 1970, in his ninety-eighth year.

Russell's Philosophy of Logic

ii

For all that contemporary philosophers owe to him, Russell's conception of philosophy is old-fashioned. I have already spoken of him as a figure in the high tradition of British empiricism: and in fact he stands much closer to Locke and Berkeley and Hume and John Stuart Mill than he does to the followers of Moore or Wittgenstein or Carnap. The main reason for this is that he makes the now unfashionable assumption that all our beliefs are in need of philosophical justification. He does not, indeed, suppose that any philosophical argument could be sufficient to settle such empirical questions as the existence of the table at which I believe myself to be writing or the outcome of the Battle of Waterloo, or even such formal questions as the existence of an even prime number or the validity of Pythagoras's theorem, but he does take it to be necessary. The reason why he takes it to be necessary is that in answering any such questions we assert propositions which we are not entitled to accept unless we are entitled to believe that certain types of entity exist. There cannot be tables unless there are physical objects; there cannot be battles unless there are men who fight them and places and times at which they are fought; there have to be numbers for any numbers to be prime; unless there are right-angled Euclidean triangles, there cannot be any relation between the squares of their hypotenuses and the squares of their other two sides. But whether, and in what sense, we can be justified in thinking that there are physical objects, or persons, or points in space, or past events, or numbers, or Euclidean triangles is, in each instance, as Russell sees it, a matter for philosophical debate.

But how should such a debate proceed? Russell's answer to this question goes back to Descartes. We are to start with the elements which are the least susceptible to doubt and then see what can be constructed out of them, or inferred from them. In Russell's system, as we shall see, the elements are very much the same as they were taken to be by Locke. Just as Locke started with "simple ideas of sensation" and "simple ideas of reflection,"[1] so Russell assumes that "we have acquaintance in sensation with the data of the outer senses, and in introspection with the data of what may be called the inner senses—thoughts, feelings, desires, etc.":[2] and just as Locke credited us with the power of forming abstract ideas out of the materials with which we are presented in sensation or reflection, so Russell thinks that our acquaintance extends to universals, such as

[1] John Locke, *An Essay Concerning Human Understanding*, Book II, ch. i.
[2] Bertrand Russell, *The Problems of Philosophy*, p. 51.

whiteness or diversity, which are exemplified in our experience, or at least are analyzable into terms which are so exemplified. As Russell puts it, "Every complete sentence must contain at least one word which stands for a universal, since all verbs have a meaning which is universal."[3] These universals are either qualities or relations, and it is by truly predicating a quality of a presented object, or a relation between two or more of them, that we arrive at the basic facts upon which all our empirical knowledge must be founded.

Even at this early stage we encounter philosophical problems. There is the problem of the range of the basic facts and there are problems about the way in which they are to be interpreted. What, for example, is the status of the primitive data of sense? Are they private or public, mental or physical, or do these categories not apply to them? We shall see that Russell takes them to be private but not mental.[4] Then again, he has provisionally admitted the distinction between particulars and universals, and that between qualities and relations, but it may be doubted whether these distinctions are ultimate. There are philosophers who have denied the reality of universals and there are those who have denied the existence of relations, in the sense that they have treated all propositions as being of the subject-predicate form. This, indeed, was the view that Russell attributed to Leibniz, in the book which he devoted to Leibniz's philosophy, and he held it to be responsible for the salient features of Leibniz's metaphysics. He himself is quite clear that a proposition which asserts a relation between two terms cannot be legitimately equated with a proposition which implies the existence of only one of them, and accordingly concludes that some propositions

[3] *Ibid.*, p. 52.
[4] See below, pp. 69–71.

are irreducibly relational. He also holds, as we shall see,[5] that there are no valid means of eliminating universals. On the other hand, as we shall also see,[6] he is not so easily satisfied with the assumption of particulars. Like Locke, he is suspicious of the concept of substance; but whereas Locke felt bound to admit the existence of a something he knew not what[7] which held qualities together, we shall find that Russell eventually came to take the view, against which he had previously argued, that particulars can be replaced by complexes of qualities.

The question about the range of basic facts is also one about which Russell held different opinions at different times. At the time that he wrote *The Problems of Philosophy* he held that the exercise of memory could afford us direct acquaintance with our past experiences, but later, in his *Analysis of Mind*, he takes the view that any belief which is founded on memory must be inferential, and to that extent uncertain.[8] Again, having maintained, with some hesitation, in *The Problems of Philosophy* that one can be acquainted with one's self, at least as the momentary owner of the experiences that one is currently having, he first switches to the view that one has knowledge of one's self, as an entity distinct from one's experiences, not by acquaintance but only by description, as whatever it may be that owns the experiences,[9] and then, in *The Analysis of Mind* decides that there is no need to regard the self as a

[5] See below, p. 105.
[6] See below, p. 107.
[7] See John Locke, *An Essay Concerning Human Understanding*, Book II, ch. xxiii.
[8] See below, p. 89.
[9] See the essay "On the Nature of Acquaintance" (1914) reprinted in *Logic and Knowledge*.

separate entity from its experiences, since it can be constructed out of them. The same progressive tendency toward economy is shown in his treatment of abstract entities. We shall see that the generous Platonism of *The Principles of Mathematics*, in which reality was conceded to every object of thought, is pared away to the point where even such comparatively respectable abstract entities as classes and propositions appear as logical fictions, and we are left only with universals, and perhaps also with facts, though Russell's final view appears to have been that facts also are eliminable in favor of those complexes of qualities which he calls events.

This is not, or not just, love of economy for its own sake. The reason for Russell's fidelity to Ockham's razor, the principle that entities are not to be unnecessarily multiplied, is that the more entities you postulate, the greater is the risk of your believing in something that does not exist. A position of complete skepticism is not practically tenable: we cannot divest ourselves of what Hume called our natural beliefs; but we may be able to reformulate these beliefs in such a way as to increase their security without too seriously impoverishing their content. Thus, in the case of one's self, one will not accept a theory which results in the denial, or even in any serious doubt of one's own existence; but if the self can be analyzed in terms of its experiences, one's belief in one's own existence acquires a more solid basis than if one were to identify one's self with anything so dubious as a spiritual substance. In the case of propositions, we do not want to deny that sentences can have a meaning, but we may be able to account for this in a more informative and less speculative way than by postulating the existence of a special class of entities which they mean. In relation to numbers, Russell once spoke of postulation as having "the advantages of theft over honest toil"[10]; but his objection to it is not primarily that it is a mark of philosophical laziness: it is rather that it gives unnecessary hostages to fortune.

The same principle of caution governs Russell's extension of his primary data. He sees that no credible picture of the world can be fashioned solely out of one's own experiences, even if one adds the deliverances of memory to those of present sensation and introspection. The question is how these fragmentary materials are to be supplemented. Now, in going beyond a given set of elements, there are two kinds of inferences that one can make. The entities to which one infers can be of the same sort as those with which one starts or they can be of a different sort. Let us call inferences of the first kind horizontal inferences and those of the second kind vertical inferences. Russell's principle is that the resources of the horizontal type of inference should be exhausted before we have recourse to the vertical. Thus, we shall see that he tries to exhibit physical objects as consisting of elements of the same character as the data of sense, and that it is only because he feels that the result is not scientifically adequate that he shifts to conceiving of them as the unobserved causes of our percepts. Again, at a level where he is taking the existence of physical objects as established, he urges that there is no need to make a vertical inference to the existence of points and instants; they can be represented as classes of physical volumes and events.[11] To assume that there are volumes, or events, which have the requisite relations to one another may, indeed, itself be a step which takes us beyond our data, but the point is that it does not take us to another level. It is not a passage to what Russell

[10] *Introduction to Mathematical Philosophy*, p. 71.
[11] See *Our Knowledge of the External World*, Lecture IV.

would call an inferred entity. For an inferred entity, in his usage, is always the product of a vertical inference.

The principle which I have just explained is one that Russell himself expresses more succinctly. "The supreme maxim in scientific philosophising is this: Wherever possible, logical constructions are to be substituted for inferred entities."[12] An object A is shown to be a logical construction out of a set of objects B, C, D, when some rule can be given for translating any statement about A into a set of statements about B, C, D, which have at least the same factual content. Since the entities which Russell wishes to exhibit as logical constructions already play an important role in our system of beliefs, the process of constructing them assumes the form of a process of analysis: and for this reason Russell is often represented as being primarily an analytical philosopher. Nevertheless it is quite clear from his writings that he is not interested in analysis for its own sake. For him, it is always the inverse process of construction, and thus an attempt to give greater security to beliefs that would otherwise be more problematic. In short, he uses analysis as a method of justification.

B. THE REDUCTION OF MATHEMATICS TO LOGIC

The point which I have just been making comes out clearly in Russell's philosophy of mathematics. Here again, he starts with the assumption that the existence of the abstract entities to which purely arithmetical propositions apparently refer is a legitimate subject for doubt. As he himself puts it, "Two equally numerous collections appear to have something in common: this something is supposed to be their cardinal number. But so long as the cardinal number is inferred from the col-

[12] "Sense-data and Physics," in *Mysticism and Logic*, p. 155.

lections, not constructed in terms of them, its existence must remain in doubt, unless in view of a metaphysical postulate *ad hoc*. By defining the cardinal number of a given collection as the class of all equally numerous collections, we avoid the necessity of this metaphysical postulate, and thereby remove a needless doubt from the philosophy of arithmetic."[13] The method by which this definition is effected was first discovered by the German logician Gottlob Frege, but Russell hit upon it independently, and it was through Russell that Frege's work became generally known, over twenty years after it was first published.

The idea being that a number is a class of equally numerous classes, the problem is to determine without circularity when two classes are equally numerous. This is effected by means of the concept of a one-one relation. A relation between two terms x and y is said to be one-one when no other term than x is so related to y and x is so related to no other term than y. When only the first of these conditions is fulfilled, the relation is said to be one-many: when only the second is fulfilled, the relation is said to be many-one. Thus, to use one of Russell's examples, in a family where there is more than one son, the relation of father to son is one-many, and that of son to father many-one, but the relation of father to eldest son is one-one.[14] Now in any case in which two classes C and D have the same number of elements, it is assumed that a relation can be discovered or devised which will be such that it correlates each element of C one to one with an element of D. When this has been achieved the two classes are said to be similar. The number of a class can then be identified with the class of those classes that are similar to it, and

[13] *Ibid.*, p. 156.
[14] *Introduction to Mathematical Philosophy*, p. 15.

a number can be identified in general as anything which is the number of some class. Since the number of a class has already been defined without reference to number, this definition will not be circular.

To say that the number of a class is the class of those classes which are similar to it may give the impression that in defining any particular number, say the number two, one has to begin by specifying one of its elements, in this case some actual couple. But this is not so. A couple can be defined in purely abstract fashion as any class such that there are objects x and y which are members of it, that x is not identical with y, and that with regard to any object z, if z is a member of it, z is either identical with x or identical with y. Evidently this method can be applied to all finite classes, including the null class, which is the class such that there is no object x which is a member of it. So, starting with 0, as the class whose only member is the null class, and defining the successor of a number as the class of classes which contain a term in addition to the number of those contained in the classes which are members of its predecessor, we can generate the whole series of natural numbers, provided that we can allot every number a successor and no two numbers the same successor. The fulfillment of these conditions is taken for granted in arithmetic, but they create a difficulty for Russell, since he has to make sure that there exist classes with enough members to generate any given number. If the supply were to give out, we should be left with a number which had only a series of zeros for its progeny. In the case of finite integers, relying on the fact that there are 2^n classes of n individuals and that 2^n is always greater than n, we can avoid this disaster by starting with classes of individuals, or classes of classes of individuals, and so on, up to the number required: but for special reasons this device is not available for classes which have an infinite number of members. Since such classes are needed in mathematics in order to define real numbers, and for other purposes, Russell has to introduce a special axiom, the so-called Axiom of Infinity, according to which "If n be any inductive cardinal number, there is at least one class of individuals having n terms."[15] It is, however, hard to see how this can be represented as a logical truth.

By making use of the concept of the similarity of relations, which is analogous to that of the similarity of classes, Russell is able to deal with ordinal numbers, and the definition in logical terms of rational, real, and complex numbers is then fairly easily accomplished. Neither does he encounter any difficulty of principle in extending the mantle of logic over those branches of mathematics which are not deducible from the theory of the natural numbers. Geometry is accommodated by being treated as a purely formal affair, with no especial reference to space. The primitive terms of a geometrical system can be equated with anything that satisfies its axioms, and what the system assures us is that anything which satisfies the axioms will also satisfy the theorems. Thus, on one interpretation of Euclidean geometry, a point becomes identical with a triad of real numbers,[16] and this is just as legitimate as its identification with a class of volumes. This is not to deny the historical connection of geometry with the measurement of space; but the question whether Euclidean or some other form of geometry finds an adequate interpretation in the actual character of physical space is, in Russell's view, a scientific question, the answer to which is independent of the

[15] *Introduction to Mathematical Philosophy*, p. 131.
[16] See Jean Nicod, *Foundations of Geometry and Induction*, pp. 7–8.

validity of these geometries, considered merely as formal systems.

As I have said, the system of logic out of which mathematics was to be generated was developed by Russell and Whitehead in their *Principia Mathematica*. The system is extensional, in the sense that the replacement within it of one proposition by another which has the same truth-value always leaves the truth-value of the proposition in which the replacement occurs unchanged. The propositional calculus with which it starts contains four logical operators, called by Russell logical constants, which are those of negation, conjunction, disjunction, and implication, and all of them are definable in terms of truth-values. Thus, the negation of any proposition p is a proposition which is true when p is false and *vice versa*; the conjunction of p and another proposition q is a proposition which is true just in case both p and q are true; the disjunction of p and q is a proposition which is true when either p or q or both are true; and the implication of q by p, the proposition that if p then q, is true just in case either p is false or q is true. The objection, which is sometimes made, that this is not what we ordinarily mean by "if . . . then" is correct, but irrelevant. The most it proves is that the symbol "$\supset$" which Russell uses for implication should not be rendered as "if . . . then" in English: it does not prove that the interpretation which he gives to it is not adequate for his purpose. It is in any case dispensable since it was later shown by H. M. Sheffer, and had indeed been previously discovered by C. S. Peirce, that the four logical constants can be replaced by one, the so-called stroke-function, which can be interpreted either as yielding a proposition which is true just in case not both p and q are true, or as yielding a proposition which is true just in case both p and q are false. When it comes to the predicate calculus, which is especially important for the derivation of mathematics, the list of logical constants is augmented by the introduction of what are known as quantifiers. The notion of a quantifier is linked with that of a propositional function. As Russell defines it, a propositional function is "an expression containing one or more undetermined constituents, such that, when values are assigned to these constituents, the expression becomes a proposition."[17] This definition is misleading in that it suggests that Russell treats propositions and propositional functions as symbols, whereas in fact he commonly identifies them with what the symbols in question symbolize, but apart from that it serves its purpose. Thus, the formula "x is wise" expresses a propositional function and comes to express a proposition when some name or description of a person is substituted for "x": the formula "f Socrates" expresses a propositional function which yields a proposition when the predicate is made determinate. The letters "x" and "f" in these formulae are said to stand for variables. Now, instead of giving particular values to the variables, we can also obtain a proposition by quantifying over them: that is, in effect, by asserting that the function is satisfied by some value or other, or that it is satisfied by all the values, of the variable in question. Russell quantifies in this way over both individuals and properties, but for the sake of simplicity let us confine ourselves to the case of individuals. Then, quantification over the variable x in the function "x is wise" yields the propositions "For some x, x is wise," *anglice* "Someone is wise" and "For all x, x is wise," *anglice* "Everyone is wise." In the first of these examples we are employing what is called the existential, and in the second what is called the universal quantifier.

[17] *Introduction to Mathematical Philosophy*, pp. 155–56.

So much for the logical constants of Russell's and Whitehead's system of logic. The system has five primitive propositions which Jean Nicod, by employing the stroke-function, later showed to be reducible to one. But this proposition is very complicated, so that it will be better to list the original five. In what follows, the signs "*p*," "*q*," and "*r*" stand for variables for which any propositions can be substituted, provided that the same substitution is made for a given variable throughout any proposition in which it occurs. Then the primitive propositions are (i) If either *p* or *p*, then *p*; (ii) If *q*, then either *p* or *q*; (iii) If *p* or *q*, then *q* or *p*; (iv) If *p* or (*q* or *r*), then *q* or (*p* or *r*), and; (v) If (if *q* then *r*) then [if (*p* or *q*) then (*p* or *r*)]. These five propositions are all employed as formal rules of inference. In addition there is need for two nonformal rules, one of them being the rule which allows the consistent substitution of any proposition, however, complex, for the *p*'s and *q*'s and *r*'s, and the other being the rule that when "*p*" and "if *p* then *q*" have been established "*q*" is to be accepted. The reason why this has to be a nonformal rule is that if we tried to achieve the same end by adopting the proposition "If [*p* and (if *p* then *q*)] then *q*" as a premise, we should require a further premise to the effect that *q* was implied by the addition of this proposition to the others and in this way, as Lewis Carroll showed,[18] we should embark upon an infinite regress. These then are the simple foundations upon which the whole of propositional logic can be built.

Russell says comparatively little about the status which he attributes to the propositions of logic themselves. In his earlier works, he rejects the received view that true propositions of logic are analytic, mainly on

[18] Lewis Carroll, "What the Tortoise Said to Achilles," *Mind*, IV, 278.

the ground that this would make them trivial, and prefers to characterize them in terms of their complete generality, or by the fact that they are true solely in virtue of their form. Later on, he came to share Wittgenstein's view that the truths of the propositional calculus are tautologies, in the technical sense that they remain true whatever truth-values are assigned to their constituents. With regard to the truths of logic which do not fall within the propositional calculus, he seems to have held that they were analytic after all, in the not entirely clear sense of their being true in virtue of nothing other than the meaning of the symbols which express them. Russell does not discuss the problem how we can then avoid the conclusion that mathematics is trivial, but the only answer which would appear to be open to him is that it would be trivial for a being who could immediately grasp all the implications of any set of definitions, and that it is not trivial for us only because we are not in this position. This answer is, however, open to the objection that to draw the consequences of a set of definitions is itself an exercise in logic.

C. THE THEORY OF TYPES

As we have seen, Russell's reduction of mathematics to logic has the effect of eliminating numbers in favor of classes. This is anyhow a gain in economy, but it will not be a sufficient gain in clarity so long as the notion of a class is itself problematic. It might seem that we could take the easy way of treating classes extensionally, as collections of objects which we could in principle enumerate, so that all that we should need to understand would be the simple process of conjunction, but this approach encounters unexpected difficulties. For example, we may have to deal with classes which have an infinite number of members, and it is hard to accept the notion of an infinite conjunction: neither is it easy to see how the null class can be a collection. Moreover, it seems absurd to think of a collection as an entity distinct from the items which compose it, so that when one buys a pair of shoes, one is buying three things, the right shoe, the left shoe, and the pair. Not only that, but if we do conceive of classes as entities and also make what would then seem the reasonable assumption that they are to be included in the totality of the things that there are, we fall into contradiction. This comes about through the fact, to which we have already referred, that given any set of n objects one can make 2^n different selections from them, and that even in the case where n is infinite, 2^n is greater than n. For then if we take n to be the total number of things, and include in this totality the number of possible selections that can be made from it, we arrive at the self-contradictory result that the number of things that there are is greater than their totality. As Russell puts it, we have "a perfectly precise arithmetical proof that there are *fewer* things in heaven and earth than are dreamt of in *our* philosophy."[19]

For these reasons Russell prefers to treat classes intensionally as the sets of objects which satisfy such and such propositional functions; so that, for example, the class of men is equated with the set of objects which yield true values for the function "x is a man." This enables him to eliminate classes, in the sense that every statement about a class can be represented as a statement about a corresponding propositional function. There is a difficulty arising from the fact that more than one function may determine the same class, as, for example, the class of men is also the class of featherless

[19] "The Philosophy of Logical Atomism," in *Logic and Knowledge*, p. 260.

bipeds, but this can be overcome. Even so, a serious problem remains. It is natural to suppose that every propositional function determines a class, even if it be only the null class, and in some cases the class in question may be one which has classes for its members, though Russell makes the assumption that functions which range over classes are in the end replaceable by functions which range over individuals. But now it turns out that unless we place some restriction on the ranges of our functions, we again fall into contradiction. The example which Russell discovered is that of predicating of a class that it is or is not a member of itself. For instance, it seems reasonable to say, on the one hand, that the class of things which can be counted is itself something that can be counted, and, on the other, that the class of men is not itself a man. In this way we seem to obtain two classes of classes: the class of classes which are members of themselves and the class of classes which are not members of themselves. But now if we ask with respect to this second class of classes whether or not it is a member of itself, we get the contradictory answer that if it is, it is not, and if it is not, it is. It was the discovery of this contradiction that obstructed Russell in the composition of *Principia Mathematica*, and it was taken no less seriously by Frege, who said, when Russell told him of it in a letter, that the foundations of mathematics had been undermined.

Russell's attempt to find a solution to this antinomy, and also to other antinomies like that of Epimenides the Cretan, who said that all Cretans were liars, resulted in what is known as his Theory of Types. This theory has ramifications into which I shall not enter here, but in its simplest form it lays down the principle that the meaning of a propositional function is not specified until we specify the range of objects which are candidates for satisfying it. From this it follows that these candidates cannot meaningfully include anything which is defined in terms of the function itself. So Russell's solution of his paradox is that to say of the class of classes which are not members of themselves that it either is, or is not, a member of itself is neither true nor false but meaningless. By applying this principle he arrives at a system in which propositional functions, and consequently propositions, are arranged in a hierarchy. At the lowest level we have functions which range only over individuals, then come functions which range over functions of the first order, then functions which range over functions of the second order, and so on. Objects which are candidates for satisfying functions at a given level are said to constitute a type, and the rule is that what can be said, truly or falsely, about objects of one type cannot meaningfully be said about objects of a different type. When it is expressed in this way, the rule appears to commit one to admitting the existence of more kinds of objects than Russell would be willing to countenance, but it is easy to see that this commitment can be avoided by rephrasing his principle in the form of a rule as to what combinations of symbols are to be regarded as significant. Since there will be an order of propositions, corresponding to the order of propositional functions, it follows, among other things, that we cannot significantly attribute any property to propositions in general, but only at best to propositions of such and such an order. So Epimenides the Cretan could not meaningfully have said that all propositions which were asserted by Cretans were false but only, at best, that all propositions of order n which were asserted by Cretans were false; and since this would itself be a proposition of a higher order than n, no paradox arises.

To this extent, the theory achieves its purpose, but it

is arguable that it is too stringent. One difficulty which troubled Russell is that it is sometimes necessary in mathematics to make propositions about all the classes that are composed of objects of any one logical type. But then the obstacle arises that the functions which a given object is capable of satisfying may not themselves be all of the same type: there may be some among them which refer to some totality of the others, as in Russell's example "Napoleon had all the qualities of a great general," where "having all the qualities of a great general" is not itself a quality of the same type as the qualities it indicates, which must also be ascribable to Napoleon if this proposition is true.[20] Now, there is no objection to our asserting severally of a set of functions of different types that they are satisfied by the same object, but we violate the theory of types when we try to attribute to the object the property of satisfying the totality of these functions; for according to the theory, no such totality can significantly be spoken of. Russell's solution of this difficulty is to assume the so-called Axiom of Reducibility. He says that two functions are formally equivalent when they are satisfied by the same objects: he speaks of any object for which a function has the value of truth or falsehood as an argument of the function; and he calls a function predicative when it does not involve reference to any collection of functions. Then, the Axiom of Reducibility is that with regard to any function F which can take a given object A as argument, there is some predicative function, also having A among its arguments, which is formally equivalent to F. Clearly, this axiom does meet the difficulty, but again Russell does not succeed in proving that it is a logical truth.

[20] *Introduction to Mathematical Philosophy*, pp. 189–90.

A simpler reason for thinking that the theory of types may be too stringent is that there are many cases in which we do seem able to make the same statement significantly about objects of different types. For instance, we can count objects at different levels, yet we do not credit numerical expressions with a different meaning according as they are applied to classes with elements of different sorts. Russell's answer to this is that they do, indeed, have a different meaning in these different applications. Expressions which we seem able to apply without trouble to objects of different types are said by him to be "systematically ambiguous." It is because the ambiguity is systematic that it escapes our notice. The fact remains, however, that but for the theory of types, we should not be inclined to think in these cases that there was any ambiguity at all.

Because of such difficulties, many logicians have chosen to dispense with the theory of types and try to find some other way of dealing with the paradoxes which it was designed to meet. For instance, there are those who hold that the class paradox can be avoided by depriving it of its subject: there just is no class of classes which are not members of themselves. The theory has, on the other hand, had a considerable influence outside the field of strictly formal logic. It helped to give currency to the view, which was taken up enthusiastically by the Logical Positivists in the 1930s in their onslaught on metaphysics, that sentences to which there is no obvious objection on the score of grammar and vocabulary may nevertheless be meaningless; and together with Russell's Theory of Descriptions it encouraged philosophers to distinguish the grammatical form of a sentence from what Russell called its logical form, and thereby gave a strong impetus to the practice of philosophical analysis.

D. THE THEORY OF DESCRIPTIONS

An assumption which Russell makes in *The Principles of Mathematics* and elsewhere is that the meaning of a name is to be identified with the object which the name denotes. It is thereby made a necessary though not a sufficient condition for anything to be named that it be capable of being denoted. In the period of his Platonism, when *The Principles of Mathematics* was written, Russell interpreted this condition very liberally. Anything that could be mentioned was said by him to be a term: any term could be the logical subject of a proposition; and anything that could be the logical subject of a proposition could be named. It followed that one could in principle use names to refer not only to any particular thing that exists at any place and time, but to abstract entities of all sorts, to nonexistent things like the present Tsar of Russia, to mythological entities like the Cyclops, even to logically impossible entities like the greatest prime number. Not only that, but Russell also held that expressions like "all men," "every man," "any man," "a man," "some man," all denoted separate objects, which were distinct from one another and from the abstract object which was denoted by the word "humanity."

It was not very long, however, before Russell came to think that this picture of the world was intolerably overcrowded. Even before he took the view that classes were logical fictions, he ceased to find it credible that to speak of the members of a class collectively and to speak of them severally was to speak of different objects, and that an expression like "any man" could denote an object which was distinct from any man in particular. He also found himself unable any longer to believe in the being of logically impossible entities or even in that of possible things which were known not to exist. His comment on his earlier theory was that it showed "a failure of that feeling for reality which ought to be preserved even in the most abstract studies.[21] Logic," he continues, "must no more admit a unicorn than zoology can; for logic is concerned with the real world just as truly as zoology, though with its more abstract and general features."[22] Neither can there be any world, other than the real world, in which such things as unicorns, or golden mountains, or the greatest prime number could be found.

It was, however, not only the growth in his feeling for reality that led Russell to look for a different account of denotation. He found that the position which he had adopted in *The Principles of Mathematics* raised problems to which it could not supply an answer. Some of these problems are set out in an article, "On Denoting," which first appeared in *Mind* in 1905 and is reprinted in *Logic and Knowledge*. For example, if denoting phrases like "the author of *Waverley*" function as names, and if the meaning of a name is identical with the object which it denotes, it will follow that what is meant by saying that Scott was the author of *Waverley* is simply that Scott was Scott. Yet it is surely obvious, as Russell remarks, that when George IV wished to know whether Scott was the author of *Waverley*, he was not expressing an interest in the law of identity. Again, if the phrase "the present King of France" denotes a term, and if the law of excluded middle holds, one or other of the two propositions "The present King of France is bald" and "The present King of France is not bald" must be true. Yet if one were to enumerate all the things that are bald and all the things that are not bald, one would not find the present King of France

[21] *Introduction to Mathematical Philosophy*, p. 169.
[22] *Ibid.*

on either list. Russell remarks characteristically that "Hegelians, who love a synthesis, will probably conclude that he wears a wig."[23] Indeed, we run into trouble even in saying that the present King of France does not exist. We seem to be required to attribute being to a term as a condition of denying its existence. The question is "How can a nonentity be the subject of a proposition?"[24]

Evidently, the main source of these difficulties is Russell's assumption that denoting phrases have the properties which he attributes to names. He therefore has the choice of looking for a different theory of the use of names, or dropping this troublesome assumption. In fact, he takes the second course. His theory of descriptions is designed to show that expressions which are classifiable as definite or indefinite descriptions are not used as names, inasmuch as it is not necessary for them to denote anything, in order to have a meaning. Or rather, since he concludes that expressions of this kind have no meaning in isolation, his argument is better put by saying that it is not necessary for them to denote anything in order that they should contribute in the way that they do to the meaning of the sentences into which they enter. Such expressions are said by Russell to be "incomplete symbols," and what he means by saying of an expression that it is an incomplete symbol, apart from its not needing to have a denotation, is that the meaning of any sentence in which it occurs can be spelled out in such a way that the resulting sentence no longer contains the expression or any synonym for it. Accordingly, what is required of the theory of descriptions is that it should provide the machinery for han-

[23] *Logic and Knowledge*, p. 48.
[24] *Ibid.*

dling descriptive phrases in such a way that they are shown to be incomplete symbols in this sense.

In the earliest version of the theory, which is set out in the article "On Denoting," and repeated, anachronistically, in the *Introduction to Mathematical Philosophy*, this machinery is a little complicated. Russell starts with the concept of a propositional function's being always true, that is to say, its being true for all the values of the variable. Let us suppose that the function has the form fx. Then the sentence "Everything has the property f" is taken to mean just that "fx" is always true. "Nothing has f" is taken to mean that "'fx' is false" is always true, and "Something has f" is taken to mean that it is false that "'fx' is false" is always true, a definition for which "'fx' is sometimes true" can be used as an abbreviation. At this point it is easy to see how we can deal with indefinite descriptions. To say, for example, that some human being has walked on the moon is to say that the propositional function "x is human and has walked on the moon" is sometimes true, or in other words, true for at least one value of x. When it comes to definite descriptions, there is the further complication that we have to stipulate that the function is true for only one value of the variable. This is achieved by adding the rider that it is always true of any object y that if y satisfies the function in question, y is identical with x. So the translation of "Scott was the author of *Waverley*" is "It is sometimes true of x (that x wrote *Waverley*, that it is always true of y that if y wrote *Waverley* y is identical with x, and that x is identical with Scott)."

In *Principia Mathematica*, this whole procedure is very much simplified by the use of quantifiers. Instead of "'fx' is always true" we can say "For all x, fx": instead of "'fx' is false' is always true" we can say "For all x, not fx" and instead of "'fx' is sometimes true" we can

say "For some x, fx" or "There is an x such that fx."
Then "Some human being has walked on the moon" becomes "There is an x such that x is human and has
walked on the moon," and "Scott was the author of
Waverley" becomes "There is an x such that x wrote
Waverley, such that, for all y, if y wrote *Waverley*, y is
identical with x, and such that x is identical with Scott."
The use of quantifiers not only simplifies the translation
but also avoids the undesirable implication of Russell's
earlier formulae that whenever we use a descriptive
phrase we are speaking in metalinguistic fashion *about*
propositional functions and the extent to which they
are satisfied.

With the introduction of quantifiers, it also becomes
clear that the theory itself is very simple. It rests on the
premise that in all cases in which a predicate is attributed to a subject, or two or more subjects are said to
stand in some relation, that is to say, in all cases except
those in which the existence of a subject is simply
asserted or denied, the use of a description carries the
covert assertion that there exists an object which
answers to it. The procedure then is simply to make this
covert assertion explicit. The elimination of descriptive
phrases, their representation as incomplete symbols, is
achieved by expanding them into existential statements
and construing these existential statements as asserting
that some thing, or in the case of definite descriptive
phrases, just one thing, has the property which is contained in the description. Once this procedure is understood, it can be seen to be applicable not only to phrases
which are explicitly of the form "a so-and-so" or "the
so-and-so" but to any nominative sign which carries
some connotation. The connotation of the sign is taken
away from it and turned into a propositional function:
when an object is found which satisfies the function,
the same treatment is applied so that the original func-

tion is augmented by another predicate: and so the process continues until we get to the point where the subject of all these predicates is either referred to indefinite by the use of the existential quantifier or named by a sign which has no connotation at all. This is the whole technique of the theory of descriptions. Applying it is like feeding an insect which absorbs all the nourishment into its body. The body swells and swells and the head remains vestigial. All that one can say about it is that it is something to which the body is attached.

Since Russell takes the view that ordinary proper names like "Scott" or "London" do have a connotation, he is bound to treat them as implicit descriptions. In his more popular expositions of the theory he is, indeed, apt to speak as if "Scott" were a genuine proper name and to contrast it with a definite description like "the author of *Waverley*," but this is just for convenience of exposition. When he wishes to be accurate, he takes care to remark that names like "Scott" are not genuine proper names. He does not go into this question in any detail but his view appears to be that a proper name of this sort is a substitute for whatever description of its intended reference the speaker has in mind when he uses the name, or the hearer when he understands its use. As an account of the way in which such names are actually employed, this view is exposed to certain difficulties, but, as we shall see in a moment, Russell is not primarily interested in elucidating ordinary usage. Since his theory requires that any descriptive meaning which a nominative sign carries should be incorporated into a predicative sign, the only function which is left for a name to fulfill is that of being purely demonstrative. Russell calls these purely demonstrative signs logically proper names and he takes it to be characteristic of a logically proper name that its significant use guarantees the existence of the object which it is intended to denote. Since the only signs which satisfy this condition are, in his view, those which refer to present feelings or sense-data, his philosophy of logic is tied at this point to his theory of knowledge.

An important consequence of the theory of descriptions is that existence is treated as a property of propositional functions. On this point Russell is in substantial agreement with Frege, who takes existence to be a property of concepts. This is not of course to say that they attribute existence *to* concepts, let alone exclusively to concepts, but rather that they take the attribution of existence to anything to consist in the attribution to a concept of the property of having application, or, as Russell would put it, in the attribution to a propositional function of the property of being satisfied. It follows that the kinds of objects which are said to exist will depend on the kinds of propositional functions which are said to be satisfied; and this is the source of Professor Quine's celebrated dictum that "To be is to be the value of a variable."[25] It also follows that an ascription of existence cannot significantly be coupled with the use of a logically proper name. The point here is not just that to affirm the existence of a named object would be pleonastic and to deny it self-stultifying, since we should in the one case be repeating and in the other contradicting what the use of the name presupposed: it is rather that since a logically proper name cannot be expanded into a propositional function, an object which is named in this way cannot meaningfully be said either to be or not to be. If we want to say that a named object exists, we shall have to use such a device as that of saying that it has some property or other, or that it is identical with itself.

[25] W. V. Quine, *From a Logical Point of View*, p. 15.

This conclusion of Russell's has been disputed by G. E. Moore in an article in which Moore is discussing the question whether existence is a predicate.[26] Assuming, correctly, that the demonstrative "this" is an instance of what Russell calls a logically proper name, Moore argues that one can significantly say of the object to which the demonstrative is being used to refer that it might not have existed. But to say that this might not have existed is to imply that the proposition "This does not exist" might have been true, from which it follows that the sentence "This does not exist" must be significant. But if the sentence "This does not exist" is significant, it expresses a false proposition. Consequently, the proposition that this exists is a true proposition, and from this it follows that the sentence "This exists" is also significant.

I think that this argument is valid, and that Russell is therefore mistaken in believing that existence should always be construed as a property of propositional functions. Another counter-example would be Russell's own denial of existence to what he calls logical fictions. If the proposition that classes do not exist were construed in accordance with the theory of descriptions it would have to be taken to mean that no second-order functions were satisfied, which is certainly not something that Russell wishes to hold. What he means by denying that classes exist is rather something that he would express by saying that classes are not part of the ultimate furniture of the world. However, there being ascriptions of existence which it does not cover does not derogate from the fact that Russell's analysis of one very common way in which existence is predicated is valid and illuminating.

---

[26] G. E. Moore, "Is Existence a Predicate?" *Supplementary Proceedings of the Aristotelian Society*, XV (1936).

The theory of descriptions, which was at first received very favorably, to the point of being called by F. P. Ramsey "a paradigm of philosophy,"[27] has more recently met with the objection that it does not give an accurate account of the way in which definite descriptive phrases are actually used. Thus it has been argued, notably by Professor Strawson, that in sentences like "The author of *Waverley* was Scott" or "The present King of France is bald," the existence of the object, to which the descriptive phrase purports to refer, is not implicitly asserted, but rather presupposed; so that if the object does not exist the sentence should be regarded as having been used to make not a false statement but rather one that is lacking in truth-value. The point is debatable, but if it were strictly a question of ordinary usage the balance of argument might be on Strawson's side. It is, for example, a point in his favor that we do not automatically rule a statement to be false when its intended subject is designated by a false description: we may count it as true if it is true of an object which we know to be meant and are otherwise able to identify.

Such objections, however, lose their force when it is realized that the theory of descriptions does not set out to offer exact translations of the sentences on which it operates, but rather to paraphrase them. Its method of paraphrase is to make explicit the information which is implicitly contained in the use of proper names or left to be picked up from the context. This is a point on which Russell himself is not entirely clear, partly, I think, because he uses examples in which the definite descriptive phrases secure their uniqueness of reference by incorporating proper names. If we carried his analy-

[27] F. P. Ramsey, *The Foundation of Mathematics*, p. 263 n.

sis a stage further so that instead of talking about "*Waverley*" and "France" we used identifying descriptions of the book and the country in question, we should be much less inclined to say that the sentences with which we ended were synonymous with those with which we began. This is even more obvious in the case of sentences like "The policeman showed me the way," where the identifying description has to be furnished from the context. In all such cases we shall end by supplying more information than is explicitly conveyed by the sentences which we are paraphrasing, but this does not matter so long as we are not claiming to preserve identity of meaning. It is only if it were deficient in the relevant content that the paraphrase would be inadequate.

What may seem a more serious objection is that the assumption with which Russell starts, that the meaning of a name is to be identified with the object which the name denotes, is itself incorrect. The decisive argument against it, in the case of ordinary proper names, is that the name makes the same contribution to the meaning of the sentences in which it occurs, whether the object which it purports to denote exists or not. For instance, my belief that King Arthur is a historical figure may be false, but even if it is false, what I mean by saying that King Arthur fought the Saxons remains the same. It is for this reason, indeed, that Russell takes such names to be covert descriptions. But even in the case of the demonstratives which he regards as the only genuine names, his original assumption has the unfortunate consequence that the meaning of these demonstratives varies with almost every occasion of their use. In fact, the ordinary function of words like "this" is surely not to name objects but to serve as aids to orientation. Russell himself comes round to something like this view in *An Inquiry into Meaning and Truth*, where he argues that all the logically proper names, which he characterizes as denoting what he there calls "egocentric particulars," can be defined in terms of the single demonstrative "this," and then proceeds to assign this word a constant meaning in terms of the causal conditions of its use.[28]

But now, the objection to the theory of descriptions, that it is founded on a false assumption, turns strangely to its profit. For as a result of laying upon names a condition which the signs that are ordinarily counted as names do not satisfy, it arrives at the conclusion that names in their ordinary employment are dispensable. They survive vestigially only in the form of quantified variables. If it is true, as Quine has suggested,[29] that variables themselves can be explained away, the distinction between subject and predicate is shown to be replaceable by that between demonstrative and descriptive signs; and if, as seems possible,[30] demonstrative signs are also dispensable, we are left with a purely predicative language. Since the distinction between subject and predicate corresponds to the distinction between substance and attribute, it is quite in accordance with his theory of descriptions that Russell eventually comes to the conclusion that substances can be represented as groups of compresent qualities. We shall see that his reasons for accepting this conclusion are very much the same as those that led Berkeley to say that things are bundles of qualities, so that here again he shows his fidelity to the empiricist tradition.

[28] *An Inquiry into Meaning and Truth*, p. 96.
[29] W. V. Quine, "Variables Explained Away," *Selected Logical Papers*.
[30] See my essay on "Names and Descriptions" in *The Concept of a Person*.

E. RUSSELL'S THEORIES OF BELIEF AND OF TRUTH

We have seen that the system of *Principia Mathematica* is extensional, and there are signs, at least in Russell's later work, of his thinking that it ought to be possible for us to manage generally without the use of any but extensional functions. An obvious objection to this thesis, as he sees, is presented by our use of expressions which refer to what he calls propositional attitudes. For instance, if the proposition that A believes *p* is construed as a function of *p*, it is evidently not an extensional function: its truth-value does not remain constant when any proposition with the same truth-value as *p* is substituted for it; there are some truths that I believe and also undoubtedly some falsehoods, but I certainly do not believe every truth or every falsehood. But then, if a proposition of the form "A believes *p*" is not to be construed as a function of *p*, the question arises how it should be analyzed.

This is a question to which Russell was never able to find a wholly satisfactory answer. His original view was that belief was a mental attitude having for its object a proposition, which Russell then regarded as a genuine objective entity.[31] Having abandoned this view of propositions, on the ground that "it leaves the difference between truth and falsehood quite inexplicable"[32] besides offending his feeling for reality, he also found himself obliged to give up the view that belief consists in a relation of the mind to any single object. For if propositions are disqualified, the only plausible substi-

---

[31] See "Meinong's Theory of Complexes and Assumptions," in *Mind*, XIII (1904).
[32] "On the Nature of Truth," *Philosophical Essays*, p. 52.

tutes are facts, and they are ruled out by the possibility of false belief.

The theory to which Russell then turned is that propositions can be replaced in this role by their constituents, so that belief, or judgment as he then preferred to put it, becomes a multiple relation of the mind to several objects.[33] The relation has a "sense," in that it orders its terms in a certain fashion. When I judge that A loves B and when I judge that B loves A, the terms on which my judgment operates are the same in either case, but in the first case the relation of loving is before my mind as proceeding from A to B and in the second case as proceeding from B to A. My judgment is true if the terms in question really are related in the sense in which they are judged to be, and false if they are not.

One obvious defect in this theory is that, since the singular terms on which a judgment operates are taken to be actual individuals, it makes no provision for the case in which one believes something to be true of a subject under one description and false under another. This defect can be remedied, but only at the cost of bringing in intentional objects, which are no great improvement upon propositions. Neither does it seem to me to offer much in the way of an analysis of belief.

Russell himself gave up this theory when he ceased to believe in the existence of mental acts, his reason for this being that they were not empirically discoverable.[34] He had previously thought that they could be introspected, but decided that he had been misled by the grammatical form of expressions like "I believe." Having wrongly assumed that the "I" stood for an entity with which he was acquainted, he had taken the same naïve view of words which seemed to stand for its activ-

[33] *Ibid.* See also *The Problems of Philosophy*, pp. 126–28.
[34] See *The Analysis of Mind*, p. 18.

ities. In the attempt to analyze belief, he now brings back propositions, but conceives of them as furnishing the contents of beliefs. "The content of a belief," he says, "may consist of words only, or of images only, or of a mixture of the two, or of either or both together with one or more sensations."[35] In the case where the content consists only of words, he calls it a word-proposition, and in the case where it consists only of images, he calls it an image-proposition. In either form, a proposition which expresses a belief refers to the fact which Russell calls the objective of the belief in question. I shall explain later what provision he makes in the theory for differentiating between true and false belief.

As for this analysis of belief, Russell sees that it needs to be taken further. To say that someone is in a state of believing that something is so must be to say something more than that such and such a sequence of words or images is occurring in his mental history. Russell's suggestion is that belief is "constituted by a certain feeling or complex of sensations attached to the content believed";[36] and he tries to explain how variations in the accompanying feelings or sensations can account for the differences in the three kinds of belief which he classifies respectively as memory, expectation, and bare assent. At the same time he sees that it is not sufficient that the content and the belief-feeling should merely coexist. "It is necessary," he says, "that there should be a specific relation between them, of the sort expressed by saying that the content is believed."[37] Unfortunately, we are given no account of what this relation is.

Without such an account, it has to be admitted that the theory is not very informative. One obvious lacuna

[35] *Ibid.*, p. 236.
[36] *Ibid.*, p. 250.
[37] *Ibid.*

in it is that assenting to a proposition cannot simply be equated with having any sort of feeling toward a set of words or images considered in themselves. The words, or images, have to be interpreted as signs, and what one then assents to is not the signs themselves but what they signify. But then all the old problems about intentional objects reappear. It can, indeed, be argued that assent does ultimately figure in the analysis of belief as no more than the favorable reception of certain signs, considered merely as marks or noises. But then this analysis will have to incorporate some nonintentional account of the functioning of signs.

Russell tries to meet this demand in *An Inquiry into Meaning and Truth*. His definition of a sign is that "a class of events S is, for an organism O, a *sign* of another class of events E when, as a result of acquired habit, the effects of a member of S on O are (in certain respects and with certain limitations) those which a member of E had before the habit in question was acquired."[38] Propositions are now reduced to "psychological occurrences of certain sorts," which sentences are rather mysteriously said to signify but not to assert, and it is suggested that the only adequate definition of belief may be a causal one. Russell's elementary sketch of such a definition is that "We may say that two states are instances of the same belief when they cause the same behaviour," this being understood, in the case of those who possess language, to "include the behaviour that consists in uttering a certain sentence."[39]

I think that a position of this kind is tenable, but it needs to be much further elaborated. For instance, the theory that signs are substitute stimuli is evidently false if it is stated without qualification. Even in the simplest

[38] *An Inquiry into Meaning and Truth*, p. 185.
[39] *Ibid.*, p. 189.

and most favorable case, where a sign is used to refer to something which one could, if the right conditions were fulfilled, be currently experiencing, the effect of perceiving the sign is not likely to be the same in all respects as that of perceiving the object which it signifies. For one thing, it makes all the difference whether the person who interprets the sign merely envisages the object or believes that it is present: for it is only when the use of a sign arouses or expresses a belief in the presence of the object which it signifies that it tends to act as a substitute stimulus. But then it may be objected that we fall into a circle, on the ground that one needs already to understand the sign in order to have the belief. This objection may not be fatal, but to meet it effectively one will need a more sophisticated theory of meaning. In the same way, while it may be possible to work out a behavioral theory of belief,[40] it will need to take a more subtle form than that of saying that two states are instances of the same belief when they cause the same behavior. Indeed, in view of the differences that there are in people's purposes and characters, it may well happen both that the same belief issues in different behavior, and that the same behavior issues from different beliefs. This may be true not only of different people but of the same person at different times. Moreover, the influence on a person's behavior of the other beliefs that he holds has also to be taken into account.

The changes in Russell's theory of belief are matched at every point by changes in his theory of truth. When he thought of belief as a mental attitude which was directed upon propositions, conceived as objective entities, he held truth and falsehood to be indefinable attributes of such propositions. "Some propositions are

[40] See my *The Origins of Pragmatism*, pp. 40–49.

true and some false," he said, "just as some roses are red and some white,"[41] a view which has the merit of simplicity but the demerit of overlooking the fact that it is what actually goes on in the world that makes empirical propositions true or false. When he came to think of belief as a relation between the mind and a multiplicity of objects, he adopted what he rather misleadingly described as a correspondence theory of truth. The description is misleading in that to talk of correspondence is normally to imply that there are two sets of entities between which some relation holds. We have, however, seen that in Russell's theory the constituents of judgments were taken to be the very same objects as the constituents of facts. The only correspondence that there could be was between the arrangement of objects in a judgment and their arrangement in reality, so that when the judgment was true, the correspondence became an identity and the only difference between the judgment and the fact lay in the addition of a relation to the mind.

Later on, however, when he turned propositions into the contents of beliefs, Russell did come to hold a correspondence theory of truth, in the most literal sense of the term. As we have seen, he divided propositions, in this sense, into the two classes of word-propositions and image-propositions. Word-propositions could be either positive or negative, but image-propositions could only be positive. The reason for this was that whereas one could, in a favorable instance, express the proposition that an object A stood in the relation R to another object B by having an image of A standing in the relation R to an image of B, one could not express the negation of this proposition by having an image of A which failed to stand in the relation R to an image of

[41] "Meinong's Theory of Complexes and Assumptions, p. 52.

B, since there would be nothing to show that one was denying that A and B were related by R rather than by any other relation in which the images also failed to stand. Since Russell, here following Wittgenstein, thought of the relation of correspondence as pictorial, and since it is only of image-propositions that one can plausibly say that they are in any literal sense pictures of the facts which verify them, he took image-propositions to be more basic than word-propositions. Accordingly, he said that "Word-propositions may, in simple cases, be legitimately spoken of as 'meaning' image-propositions,"[42] overlooking the fact that if the word-proposition is negative there will be no equivalent image-proposition for it to mean. He could, however, have said that the meaning of a negative word-proposition was determined by, though of course not identical with, the image-proposition which was meant by its contradictory. If a word-proposition either means or has its meaning determined by an image-proposition, in this sense, let us say that it is associated with the image-proposition. Then Russell's correspondence theory of truth is that an affirmative word-proposition is true if it is associated with a true image-proposition, that a negative word-proposition is true if it is associated with a false image-proposition, and that an image-proposition is true if and only if there is a fact which it resembles.

Russell admits that this definition of truth applies only to a limited class of propositions, but it could perhaps be shown that the propositions of this class were such that the truth of all other empirical propositions depended on them. It may also be objected that not everybody thinks in images, but here again it might be held to be sufficient that the image-propositions

---

[42] "On Propositions: What they are and how they mean," in *Logic and Knowledge*, p. 315.

should be constructible, even though they were never actually constructed. These are, however, only minor difficulties. The fatal objection to the theory is that the existence of a physical resemblance between two sets of objects can never itself be sufficient to make either of them a representation of the other. There has to be a convention according to which one of them is interpreted as signifying that there exists something which resembles it in certain respects. But then this convention will not be the only one that could have served the same purpose. There are many different methods of pictorial representation, and many methods of representation that are not pictorial. In general, the pictorial methods are not the most convenient, and even in the cases where they are more convenient, there is no ground for saying that they bring us closer to the facts. But the most important point is that even when a pictorial sign is used to make a true statement, it is not just the resemblance of the sign to what it signifies that constitutes its truth. What the resemblance determines, under the relevant convention, is the meaning of the sign. What makes the sign the expression of a true proposition is the existence of the state of affairs which it signifies, and from this point of view it is immaterial whether the sign operates through resemblance or in any other manner. So, if the correspondence theory of truth is taken literally, in the sense that correspondence is treated as a physical relation, we can only conclude that it is false.

In *The Analysis of Mind*, Russell still adhered to this false theory, to the extent of maintaining that image-propositions were made true by their resemblance to facts. However, he no longer believed that all the relations that might obtain between two imaged terms could be represented by image-propositions, his reason being that the act of comparison, which is involved in such a judgment as that the sun is brighter than the moon, "is something more than the mere coexistence of two images, one of which is in fact brighter than the other."[43] Consequently, he was led to adopt a different general theory of truth, according to which an affirmative proposition of the observational kind is true if the replacement of each word by its meaning yields a fact. This is, in effect, a reversion to his earlier theory, except that the act of judgment no longer plays a part. The main objection to it is that it suffers from the difficulties of Russell's denotative theory of meaning. To the extent that it implies that a sentence expresses a true proposition when it states a fact, it can be criticized only on the ground that it is not very illuminating.

The definition of truth which goes with the behavioral theory of meaning and belief, which Russell developed in *An Inquiry into Meaning and Truth*, is that "A sentential sign present to an organism O is *true* when, *as sign*, it promotes behaviour which would have been promoted by a situation that exists, if this situation had been present to the organism."[44] As it stands, this definition overlooks the fact that in order to promote the requisite behavior, the sign would, in general, need to be believed, and it is also open to all the objections which we have seen to hold against Russell's theory of signs as substitute stimuli. Elsewhere in the book, he says of what he calls basic propositions, which are those that purport to do no more than record the speaker's present experiences, that in their case at least "the correspondence of truth and fact is causal,"[45] but even this seems to me to be incorrect. For even if the formulation of a proposition of this kind is always caused by the fact which it records, it is still the existence of the

---

[43] *The Analysis of Mind*, p. 277.
[44] *An Inquiry into Meaning and Truth*, p. 187.
[45] *Ibid.*, p. 244.

fact in question, and not its causal relation to the propositional sign, that makes the proposition true. Russell
himself appears to recognize this when he is concerned
with propositions which are intended to predict one's
future experiences. He holds that belief in such propositions takes the form of expectation and that an expectation may be defined as being true "when it leads to
confirmation,"[46] which is tantamount to saying that it
is true just in case the expected experience occurs. He
also shows some willingness to generalize this definition,
so as to make it apply to all propositions which refer to
one's own experiences. He speaks of the possible experiences to which such propositions refer as their verifiers,
and is at times disposed to say that a proposition of this
sort is true just in case its verifier exists.

This account of truth, at least for this limited class of
propositions, seems to me to be satisfactory, so far as it
goes, though it needs to be supported by a more adequate theory of meaning. The problem which then
exercised Russell was whether the definition could be
further generalized. Could one apply it to propositions
which referred to events outside the domain of one's
own experience? Could such propositions legitimately be
said to have verifiers? Russell's answer was that they
could, on the ground that the skeptical arguments which
might lead one to give the opposite answer would end
by confining truth "to propositions asserting what I
now perceive or remember," and that "no one is willing
to accept so narrow a theory."[46] But at this point we
pass from his philosophy of logic to his theory of knowledge.

[46] *Ibid.*, p. 216.
[47] *Ibid.*, p. 305.

Russell's Theory of Knowledge

III

A. HIS THEORIES OF PERCEPTION

The starting point of Russell's theory of knowledge, as I have already said, is very much the
same as that of Locke. He takes it for granted
that all our knowledge of the world is derived
from sense-perception, and he also assumes that
"the things that are immediately known in sensation"[1] are not straightforwardly identifiable with
the physical objects which we ordinarily think
that we perceive. Where he mainly differs from
Locke is in wishing to avoid any suggestion that
these sensory elements are mind-dependent. So
where Locke had spoken of "simple ideas of
sense" he speaks of "sense-data," a term which
he probably borrowed from G. E. Moore. In *The
Problems of Philosophy*, where he first introduces the term, he gives as examples of sense-

[1] *The Problems of Philosophy*, p. 12.

data "such things as colours, smells, hardnesses, rough-
nesses and so on"[2] and distinguishes them from sensations, which he identifies with the experiences of being
immediately aware of sense-data. "Thus," he says,
"whenever we see a colour, we have a sensation *of*
the colour, but the colour itself is a sense-datum, not a
sensation. The colour is that *of* which we are immediately aware, and the awareness itself is the sensation."[3]
In *The Problems of Philosophy*, he relies on this distinction to refute Berkeley's thesis that the immediate data
of sense are ideas in the mind of the percipient. From
the fact that awareness is a state of mind, he argues that
it does not follow that the things of which one is aware
are mental, in any other but the trivial sense of being
before the mind, which is just a way of saying that they
are objects of awareness. He therefore concludes that
there is no logical reason why sense-data should not
exist independently of being sensed. If he nevertheless
thinks that they do not so exist, it is on the ground that
they are causally dependent on the bodily state of the
percipient. It is also on empirical grounds that he takes
sense-data to be private entities. Again, he sees no contradiction in supposing that two different persons are
simultaneously aware of numerically the same sense-
data, but he assumes that for this to be the case it
would be necessary both that the sense-data of which
they were respectively aware should emanate from the
same physical object, however this fact is to be analyzed,
and that they should be qualitatively identical: and
because of the differences in perspective which he
believes to arise from the fact that the two observers
cannot simultaneously occupy the same spatial position,

[2] *Ibid.*
[3] *Ibid.*

he thinks it very improbable that the sense-data ever would be qualitatively identical.

In *The Analysis of Mind*, as we have seen, Russell gives up his belief in the existence of mental acts. This is partly because of his view that the subject, to which they are ascribed, is a logical fiction, and partly, as has been said, because he has been persuaded that no such things are empirically detectable. No longer believing that there are sensations, in the sense in which he had previously used the term, he cannot *a fortiori* believe that they have any objects; and he therefore also denies that there are sense-data. But although he subsequently speaks of himself as having "emphatically abandoned"[4] sense-data at this time, the change in his view is much less radical than this would suggest. He did cease to employ the term "sense-datum," but he continued to speak of percepts, to which he attributed the same properties as he had attributed to sense-data, except that of being correlative to sensory acts.

In any case, the question which primarily interested Russell was not the relation of sense-data to the subjects whom he supposed to be aware of them, but their relation to the physical objects with which they are in some manner associated; and what he says on this score about sense-data applies equally well to percepts. Employing the familiar example of someone's perceiving a table, he says that "It is plain that if we are to know anything about the table it must be by means of the sense-data—brown colour, oblong shape, smoothness, etc.—which we associate with the table"; but, he continues, "we cannot say that the table *is* the sense-data, or even that the sense-data are directly properties of the table."[5] The reasons why he thinks that these

[4] *My Philosophical Development*, p. 245.
[5] *The Problems of Philosophy*, p. 12.

things cannot be said are drawn from what has come to be known as the argument from illusion. This argument is partly based upon the fact that an object like a table may present a different appearance to different observers, according as they look at it from different angles, or under different physical conditions, or according as they are themselves in different physical or psychological states. As Russell puts it,

Although I believe that the table is 'really' of the same colour all over, the parts that reflect the light look much lighter than the other parts, and some parts look white because of reflected light. I know that, if I move, the parts that reflect the light will be different, so that the apparent distribution of colours on the table will change. It follows that if several people are looking at the table at the same moment, no two of them will see exactly the same distribution of colours, because no two can see it from exactly the same point of view, and any change in the point of view makes some change in the way the light is reflected.[6]

Neither is it only a question of perspective. "We know," says Russell, "that even from a given point of view the colour will seem different by artificial light, or to a colour-blind man, or to a man wearing blue spectacles, while in the dark there will be no colour at all, though to touch and hearing the table will be unchanged."[7] But then what justification have we for believing that the table really is of any one particular colour? Russell's answer is that we have none. "When, in ordinary life, we speak of *the* colour of the table we only mean the sort of colour which it will seem to have to a normal spectator from an ordinary point of view under usual conditions of light. But the other colours

[6] *Ibid.*, pp. 8–9.
[7] *Ibid.*, p. 9.

which appear under other conditions have just as good a right to be considered real: and therefore, to avoid favouritism, we are compelled to deny that, in itself, the table has any one particular colour."[6]

Since the same arguments apply *mutatis mutandis* to the visible texture and shape of the table, and since he takes it to be obvious that our sensations of touch and sound "cannot be supposed to reveal *directly* any definite property of the table, but at most to be *signs* of some property which perhaps *causes* all the sensations,"[9] Russell concludes that "the real table, if there is one, is not *immediately* known to us at all, but must be an inference from what is immediately known."[10] The question then is what sort of object are we able to infer to, and how can the inference be justified?

Russell consistently adheres to the conclusion of this reasoning, but in his other writings on the topic he lays less emphasis upon the diversity of appearances which physical objects present to us, and more upon the causal dependence of any such appearances on our nervous systems and the character of our environments. Thus the fact that light, like sound, takes time to travel is invoked by him to show that when we look at an object like the sun, we do not see it in the state in which it currently is, but only, at best, in the state in which it was several minutes ago. In the case of a very remote star, it may be that at the time at which we think we see it, the star has ceased to exist. Not only that, but the evidence which goes to show that the perceptible properties, the size and shape and color, which we attribute to physical objects, appear to us as they do only because of the states of our nervous system, leaves us, in Russell's opin-

[8] *Ibid.*, pp. 9–10.
[9] *Ibid.*, p. 11.
[10] *Ibid.*

ion, with no good reason to believe that the objects possess these properties in the literal way in which they are thought to by common sense. If the attitude of common sense is represented by naïve realism, the theory that we directly perceive physical objects much as they really are, then Russell's opinion of common sense is that it simply has not kept up with the science which has developed out of it. As he succinctly puts it in *An Inquiry into Meaning and Truth*: "Naïve realism leads to physics, and physics, if true, shows that naïve realism is false. Therefore, naïve realism, if true, is false; therefore it is false."[11]

These arguments are not easy to evaluate. The fact that a table may appear a different color in different lights, or a different shape when viewed from different angles, does indeed show that our selection of one particular color, or one particular shape, as the real color, or the real shape of the table is to some extent arbitrary, but it hardly seems to warrant the conclusion that what one sees is not the table but something else. The fact that the light from a distant star may take many years to reach us does refute the naïve assumption that we see the star as a contemporary physical object, but again, it does not seem sufficient to prove that we see some contemporary object which is not the star. The evidence about the causal dependence of the way we see things on our own nervous systems is indeed harder to accommodate. If we characterize an intrinsic property of an object as one that can be adequately defined without reference to the object's effect upon an observer, then I think that a good case can be made for saying that physical objects are not intrinsically colored, though whether this entitles us to say that they are not "really" colored will still be debatable. Even so, it does not

[11] *An Inquiry into Meaning and Truth*, p. 126.

obviously follow that the color which we attribute to the table is a property of something else, a sense-datum or a percept. In all these cases we need to make two further assumptions: first, that when we perceive a physical object otherwise than as it really is, there is something we can be said to perceive directly, which really has the properties that the physical object only appears to us to have: and secondly, that what we directly perceive, in this sense, is the same whether the perception of the physical object is veridical or delusive. Russell takes these assumptions for granted, but they need to be defended. There are not many philosophers nowadays who would treat them as self-evident, if indeed they accepted them at all.

Though I myself remain in broad agreement with Russell's approach, I now think that there is an easier and safer way of obtaining what he needs for his starting point. As I have tried to show elsewhere,[12] there is a good sense in which our ordinary judgments of perception go beyond the evidence on which they are based. When I identify the object in front of me as a table, I attribute to it many properties, such as that of being tangible, of being accessible to other observers, of having a position in physical space and time, which are certainly not vouchsafed by anything in the content of my present visual experience. But then I claim that it must be possible to formulate propositions which do not in this way go beyond the evidence. The characteristic mark of such a proposition will be that it merely records the presence of a sensory pattern, without carrying any implication about the status of this pattern or about the existence or character of anything else what-

[12] See *The Origins of Pragmatism*, pp. 303–321, and "Has Austin Refuted the Sense-datum Theory?" in *Metaphysics and Common Sense*.

ever. Propositions of this kind, to which I give the name of experiential propositions, are perceptually basic, in the sense that no ordinary judgment of perception can be true unless some experiential proposition is true. I conceive of the objects which figure in these propositions as complexes of qualities, rather than as particulars in which the qualities inhere, but otherwise they are very much what Russell had in mind when he spoke of sense-data. It is, however, important to note that in speaking here of objects, I am not assigning them any special status. In particular, since neither physical objects nor persons have yet been introduced, the question whether these sensory elements are public or private, mental or physical, does not significantly arise. We shall see in a moment that his neglect of this point leads Russell into difficulties.

If we grant Russell his starting point, then the next question which arises is whether we have any good reason for regarding sense-data "as signs of the existence of something else, which we can call the physical object."[13] Russell's answer to this question in *The Problems of Philosophy* is that we do have a good if not a conclusive reason, which consists in the fact that the postulation of physical objects as external causes of our sense-data accounts for the character of the data in a way that nothing else can. These physical objects are situated by him in a space of their own which is distinct from any of the private spaces in which sense-data are located. He does not think that we can discover anything about their intrinsic properties, but does think it reasonable to infer that they are spatio-temporally ordered in a way that corresponds to the ordering of sense-data.

The postulation of physical objects is what I earlier

[13] *The Problems of Philosophy*, p. 20.

called a vertical inference,[14] and we have seen that it is one of Russell's main philosophical principles to substitute horizontal for vertical inferences, wherever this is possible. Accordingly, in *Our Knowledge of the External World*, which was published only two years after *The Problems of Philosophy*, and in two of the essays collected in *Mysticism and Logic*, he outlines a theory in which physical objects are represented as logical constructions, rather than as vertically inferred entities. For this purpose he introduces the concept of a "sensibile," with the explanation that sensibilia are objects of "the same metaphysical and physical status as sense-data,"[15] the difference being that they need not be actually sensed. Maintaining his assumption that sense-data are situated in private spaces, he takes the same to be true of sensibilia. He speaks of any two particulars which occur simultaneously in the same private space as belonging to the same "perspective," and appears to hold that sense-data which belong to different perspectives may still be located in the same space if they are sensed by the same observer. In short, he assumes, I think unwarrantably, that each observer is presented throughout his life with a single space of sight and a single space of touch, which he fuses to obtain a single private space. The private space in which a sensibile is located must presumably be constituted by the series of perspectives which would be presented to an observer who permanently occupied the appropriate point of view, but here a difficulty arises, since it is not easy to see how the point of view of a hypothetical observer can be specified except in terms of the physical space which Russell looks to his perspectives to construct.

On this basis, Russell develops a very ingenious the-

[14] See above, p. 34.
[15] *Mysticism and Logic*, p. 148.

ory, which is something along the lines of Leibniz's monadology. He looks upon each perspective as a point in what he calls "perspective-space" which, being a three-dimensional arrangement of three-dimensional perspectives, is itself a space of six dimensions. To show how this works in detail, he gives an example in which it is assumed that the same physical object appears in an indefinite number of different perspectives, the physical object being itself identified with the class of its actual and possible appearances.

> Suppose [he says], that a certain penny appears in a number of different perspectives: in some it looks larger and in some smaller, in some it looks circular, in others it presents the appearance of an ellipse of varying eccentricity. We may collect together all those perspectives in which the appearance of the penny is circular. These we will place on one straight line, ordering them in a series by the variations in the apparent size of the penny. Those perspectives in which the penny appears as a straight line of a certain thickness will similarly be placed upon a plane (though in this case there will be many different perspectives in which the penny is of the same size; when one arrangement is completed these will form a circle concentric with the penny) and ordered as before by the apparent size of the penny. By such means, all those perspectives in which the penny presents a visual appearance can be arranged in a three-dimensional spatial order.[16]

Russell then goes on to say that in each of these series a limit will be reached at the point "where (as we say) the penny is so near the eye that if it were any nearer it could not be seen."[17] If we now imagine each of them prolonged, so as to form a line of perspectives continuing

[16] *Mysticism and Logic*, p. 161.
[17] *Ibid.*, p. 162.

"beyond" the penny, the perspective in which all the lines meet can be defined as "the place where the penny is."[18]

The place *at* which a sensibile appears is then the place where the thing is of which the sensibile is an element. This is contrasted by Russell with the place *from* which the sensibile appears, which is the perspective to which the sensibile belongs. Russell says that "we may define 'here' as the place in perspective space which is occupied by our private world" and adds that this makes it possible to understand "what is meant by saying that our private world is inside our head": for the place in perspective space which our private world occupies "may be part of the place where our head is."[19] The distinction between the place at which and the place from which a sensibile appears is also used by Russell as a means of discriminating the various distances from which a thing may be perceived and of distinguishing changes in the object from changes in the environment or in the state of the observer.

Russell then proceeds to the construction of "the one all-embracing time," which he bases on "the direct time relation of before and after" obtaining between two perspectives which belong to the same person's experience. Without explaining how sensibilia are assigned to the experiences of what are only hypothetical persons, he then defines a "biography" as "everything that is (directly) earlier or later than, or simultaneous with, a given 'sensibile'" and says that "by this means, the history of the world is divided into a number of mutually exclusive biographies."[20] The correlation of the times in different biographies is achieved by starting

---

[18] *Ibid.*
[19] *Our Knowledge of the External World*, p. 92.
[20] *Mysticism and Logic*, p. 167.

with the principle that "the appearances of a given (momentary) thing in two different biographies are to be taken as simultaneous,"[21] and then modifying it in such a way as to take account of the velocities of light and sound.

There remains the problem that some sense-data are wholly delusive, such as those that occur in dreams. Here Russell consistently takes the view that there is no intrinsic difference between dreams and waking experiences. Considered in themselves, all immediate data have the same status; the propositions which record them are all equally secure. If some of them come to be dismissed as the product of total hallucination, or as merely the stuff of dreams, it is because their relations to other data are not such as to make it possible to fit them into the general scheme.

For all its ingenuity, this whole theory seems open to objection on the score of circularity. How, for example, are the perspectives which converge on the penny to be collected? Evidently, if the penny is going to be constructed out of these perspectives, it cannot itself be employed to collect them. If Russell does this, it can only be for convenience of exposition. The appearances which are taken to constitute the penny and to define its position have first to be associated on the basis of their qualities. But since different pennies may look very much alike, the only way in which we can hope to avoid mixing up sensibilia which belong to different things is by reference to the other constituents of the perspectives in which they occur. But then we encounter the difficulty that so far as our momentary fields of vision extend, the backgrounds against which different pennies are seen may themselves be qualitatively alike. To make the necessary distinctions, we shall have to refer to

[21] *Ibid.*, p. 168.

adjacent perspectives. But how are we to determine what are adjacent perspectives? The obvious course would be to define adjacency in terms of minimal overlap and to say that two perspectives overlap if and only if they contain common constituents. But how are we then to determine, in the case of unperceived perspectives, whether or not they have constituents in common?

Neither is this the only difficulty. It can also be objected that the rule by which perspectives containing appearances of the same thing are spatially ordered is not adequate for the purpose. Russell assumes that the apparent size of an object varies continuously with the distance, and its apparent shape with the angle from which the object is viewed. It is only in this way that he is able to construct his converging series. But in view of the psychological principle of constancy, this assumption is just not true to the empirical facts. It might be sustainable, if apparent sizes and shapes were assessed physiologically, but this would again incur the charge of circularity. In appealing to physiology, we should again be making use of physical objects before we had constructed them.

The main source of these difficulties, in my view, is Russell's gratuitous and indeed unwarranted assumption that sensibilia are located in private spaces. If his theory were not burdened with private spaces, there would be no need for the complex ordering of a multitude of perspectives. Instead, as I have tried to show elsewhere,[22] we can obtain the equivalent of Russell's sensibilia merely by the projection of spatial and temporal relations beyond the sense-fields in which they are originally given. Relying on the fact that similar percepts are usually obtainable at the meeting point of

[22] See *The Origins of Pragmatism*, pp. 239–41 and 322–23, and *Moore and Russell*, p. 65.

similar sensory routes, we postulate the existence at these points of what I call standardized percepts. Then, by a further inductive inference, we locate such percepts in positions which we have not actually traversed. This gives us only a skeleton of the physical world of common sense. It can, however, be given flesh by correlating the data of different senses and, at a later stage, of different observers, by separating out, as illusory, percepts which cannot be made to fit into the main pattern, and, at a later stage still, by crediting an object with causal properties. If this procedure works, we shall still not have achieved Russell's goal of exhibiting physical objects as logical constructions out of sensibilia, since there will be no question of our being able to translate propositions referring to physical objects into propositions referring only to percepts; but we shall have succeeded in exhibiting the physical world of common sense as a theory with respect to a primary world of percepts, and this in its turn as a theory with respect to the data of our experiential propositions, all without having recourse to any vertical inferences: and this I believe to be the best result that is attainable.

Russell himself makes no attempt to develop his theory any further, and indeed we soon find him tacitly reverting to his earlier theory, in which physical objects are postulated as external causes of percepts. In *The Analysis of Matter*, which was published in 1927, there are passages which suggest that he still wants to identify physical objects with groups of percepts,[23] but in the main he goes back to his old view that we know nothing about the intrinsic qualities of physical objects and that physical space is something vertically inferred, to which we are entitled to assign no more than a structural correspondence with perceptual space. What remains of his

[23] E.g., pp. 216–17.

earlier theory is the idea that the physical location of the whole of one's private visual space is inside one's own head. He now says that this follows from the causal theory of perception, which he takes to be so well established on scientific grounds that it cannot seriously be questioned. "Whoever," he says, "accepts the causal theory of perception is compelled to conclude that percepts are in our heads, for they come at the end of a causal chain of physical events leading, spatially, from the object to the brain of the percipient. We cannot suppose that, at the end of this process, the last effect suddenly jumps back to the starting-point, like a stretched rope when it snaps." Thus "What the physiologist sees when he examines a brain is in the physiologist, not in the brain he is examining."[24]

This doctrine that everything that we perceive is inside our own heads has seemed wildly paradoxical to most of Russell's critics, but it is not so very extraordinary if one accepts Russell's distinction between perceptual and physical space. For what it then comes to is the reasonable enough decision to identify the physical location of percepts with that of their immediate physical cause. What is indeed questionable is the underlying distinction, and especially its corollary that perceptual spaces are private to each percipient.

The conception of physical objects as inferred entities rather than logical constructions is still more firmly maintained in Russell's later work. Thus, in *Human Knowledge: Its Scope and Limits*, he speaks of the identification of perceptual with physical space as "a serious error committed not only by common sense but by many philosophers."[25] "The coloured surface," he then continues, "that I see when I look at a table has a

[24] *The Analysis of Matter*, p. 32.
[25] *Human Knowledge: Its Scope and Limits*, pp. 220–21.

special position in the space of my visual field; it exists only when eyes and nerves and brain exist to cause the energy of photons to undergo certain transformations. . . . The table as a physical object, consisting of electrons, positrons and neutrons lies outside my experience."[26] The most that I can know about its intrinsic properties is that they have a structural correspondence with certain of my percepts.

The great difficulty with any theory of this kind is to see how we can be justified in inferring that any such external objects exist at all. This difficulty is particularly acute for someone like Russell who holds a Humean view of causation; for if causal relations are to be analyzed in terms of observable regularities, it will seem inconsistent to ascribe causal properties to objects which are in principle unobservable. To this it may, indeed, be replied that the moral to be drawn is not that Russell's theory of perception is at fault but that his account of causation is too limited. There is no objection to the postulation of unobservable entities, so long as the hypotheses into which they enter have consequences which can be empirically tested, and it is quite customary to speak of such entities as causes of the phenomena which they are postulated to explain. But even if we accept this answer, we are still left with what seems to me the insuperable difficulty that, on Russell's theory, these unobservable objects have to be located in an unobservable space. I can conceive of there being spatial relations between unobservable objects, but only if these objects are located in a spatial system which fundamentally consists of the spatial relations which obtain between objects that are observable. I cannot see, indeed, that we have any justification for the inference that there is such a thing as unobservable space.

[26] *Ibid.*

I am not at all sure, even, that I find the concept of it intelligible.

Not only that, but the causal theory of perception, on which Russell relies, itself seems to require that physical objects be located in perceptual space. When my seeing the table in front of me is explained in terms of the passage of light rays from the table to my eye, the assumption is that the table is there when I see it, not somewhere I have no knowledge of, in a space which I do not perceive but only infer. It is true that we sometimes distinguish between the place where an object really is and the place where it appears to be. Not only is there a dislocation of time in our perception of the sun, but it seems to us much nearer than it really is. Facts of this kind are not, however, inconsistent with what I have been saying. The position of the sun is determined by calculation, and the calculations are based on the assumption that various other objects are where they appear to be. It is only because we start by equating the physical positions of things around us with the observed positions of standardized percepts that our more sophisticated methods of locating objects like the sun can lead to verifiable results.

On this point, then, I think that Russell is wrong and that common sense and the philosophers whom he criticizes for respecting it are right. It does not follow, however, that we are bound to take a naïvely realistic view of the properties of physical objects. It will still be open to us, if we choose, to regard them as really possessing only those structural properties that physicists ascribe to them. We are not even debarred from regarding percepts as private. Having developed the common-sense conception of the physical world as a theoretical system with respect to sensory qualities, we can interpret into this system the elements upon which it was founded. The physical object which was originally modeled on percepts, acquires, as it were, a life of its own. Since the perceptual qualities with which it is endowed in the theory are supposed to be constant, or at least not to change without a physical change in the object, they come to be contrasted with the fluctuating impressions which different observers have of them. The physical object into which the standardized percept has grown is thus set over against the actual percepts from which it was abstracted, and indeed regarded as causally responsible for them. A further sophistication is the replacement of the common-sense object by the scientific skeleton on which these causal processes are taken to depend. In this way, I think that a fusion of Russell's two theories of perception may lead us to the truth.

B. ON SELF-CONSCIOUSNESS AND MEMORY

We have remarked that Russell started by believing that the self was an object of acquaintance. His argument, as set out in *The Problems of Philosophy*, was based on the empirical fact that we are not only aware of things but are also, very frequently, aware of being aware of them. "When I see the sun, I am often aware of my seeing the sun; thus 'my seeing the sun' is an object with which I have acquaintance. When I desire food, I may be aware of my desire for food; thus 'my desiring food' is an object with which I am acquainted."[27] But this means that "I am acquainted with two different things in relation to each other."[28] One of them Russell takes to be a sense-datum, but what, he asks, can the other be if not myself? And if, as he supposes, we also

[27] *The Problems of Philosophy*, p. 49.
[28] *Ibid.*, p. 50.

in such cases know the truth that we are acquainted with a particular sense-datum, he does not see how we could know this truth, or even understand what is meant by it, unless we were acquainted with something which we call "I."[29] The most, however, that Russell takes this argument to prove is that one is acquainted with something which endures for at least as long as the experience in question. Some further argument will be needed to show that it exists at other times or that the self with which I am now acquainted is identical with the self with which I was acquainted a moment ago. Accordingly, he takes Descartes to task for passing immediately from the premise "I think" to the conclusion "I am a thing that thinks," but how he would himself attempt to justify a belief in the self as an enduring substance he does not say.

In *The Analysis of Mind*, as we have seen, Russell gives up this belief altogether. He there agrees with Hume that the self is not a possible object of introspection, and he thinks it naïve to suppose that just because the word "I" is used as a grammatical subject, there must be some object which it names. The general position which he adopts in this book is that the mind is constructible out of its experiences, these experiences being taken to consist, in the main, of the very same percepts as contribute to the construction of the physical world. Apart from the fact that there are also images and feelings, which enter only into the construction of minds, the difference between mind and matter is regarded not as a difference of substance or content, but as a difference in the arrangement of neutral elements. Of two groups of percepts, which may have some of their members in common, one helps to constitute a

[29] *Ibid.*, p. 51.

mind and the other a physical object, according as their members are differently related, and according as they are subject to different causal laws.

On the mental side, a theory of this sort encounters the problem of specifying the relations, whether causal or other, which have to hold between two experiences for them to be experiences of the same mind, as well as the problem of showing how the members of such a series can reflect upon one another in such a way as to account for the phenomenon of self-consciousness. It cannot be said that Russell really tackles either of these problems. He takes the obvious step of making self-consciousness through time depend on memory, without entering into any further details, and he gives only a summary account of personal identity. Thus, in his reply to his critics in *The Philosophy of Bertrand Russell*, he is content to say that "There are a number of causal con-nections between the mental occurrences which we regard as belonging to one person, which do not exist between those belonging to different people: of these memory is the most obvious and the most important."[30] He does not say what he takes these causal connections to be apart from memory, nor does he try to meet the charge of circularity which might be based on the argu-ment that one cannot discriminate the causal relations that hold between one's own experiences, unless these experiences have already been identified as one's own. He does go on to say that we must also bring in the rela-tion of compresence, "a relation which holds between any two simultaneous contents of a given mind,"[31] and should have added to it the relation of sensible con-tinuity.[32] Here too there is a suggestion of circularity,

[30] P. 699.
[31] *Ibid.*
[32] See William James, *The Principles of Psychology*, I, chap. ix.

but it can perhaps be avoided by taking these relations to be primitive. Even with these two primitive relations, memory will still be needed, because of the possibility of gaps in consciousness, and this again raises problems which Russell ignores. If we make the common assumption that the experiences which one remembers are necessarily one's own, our account of personal identity will clearly be circular. On the other hand, if we make it sufficient for anything to have been one's own experience that one seems to remember it, we may in certain cases get an unacceptable result. We shall now see that Russell's analysis of memory leaves this difficulty unsolved.

The view, which Russell held in *The Problems of Philosophy*, that memory can make us directly acquainted with past events did not survive his rejection of mental acts. It amounted in any case to little more than an unsupported claim that "memory is trust-worthy in proportion to the vividness of the experience and to its nearness in time."[33] In *The Analysis of Mind*, he starts from the fact that "everything constituting a memory-belief is happening *now*, not in the past time to which the belief is said to refer."[34] Then, since he agrees with Hume that there is no logically necessary connection between events which occur at different times, he draws the correct conclusion that "it is not logically necessary to the existence of a memory-belief that the event remembered should have occurred, or even that the past should have existed at all." "There is," he continues, "no logical impossibility in the hypothesis that the world sprang into being five minutes ago, exactly as it then was, with a population that 'remem-

[33] *The Problems of Philosophy*, p. 115, and my *The Origins of Pragmatism*, pp. 266 ff.
[34] *The Analysis of Mind*, p. 159.

bered' a wholly unreal past."[35] Consequently, "the occurrences which are *called* knowledge of the past are logically independent of the past; they are wholly analyzable into present contents which might, theoretically, be just what they are even if no past had existed."[36]

I believe that this is true and that it leads to the conclusion that no noncircular justification of memory can be given. We can check one memory-belief against another and also against historical records, our reliance on which itself depends in a large measure on memory-beliefs, but there can be no general proof that memory is reliable. In this respect it resembles induction, and indeed Russell treats it as one form of inductive inference.

There remains the question how memory is to be analyzed. Here Russell is principally concerned with what may be called occurrent as opposed to habit memory; that is to say, with the recollection of past events, rather than with displays of learning, as when one remembers a line of poetry or remembers how to perform some task. His account of occurrent memory is that it consists in the presence of an image which gives rise to a belief that something roughly corresponding to the image occurred in the past. The image has to be accompanied by what Russell calls feelings of familiarity and feelings of pastness, and the belief is one that can be expressed in the words "This existed." Russell admits that "This analysis of memory is probably extremely faulty,"[37] and indeed the conditions which he lays down appear to be neither necessary nor sufficient. They are not necessary because one can recollect a past

[35] *Ibid.*
[36] *Ibid.*, p. 160.
[37] *Ibid.*, p. 187.

experience—for instance, one's taking part in some conversation—without reproducing it in imagery, and they are not sufficient because one might hold a true belief about a past experience of one's own, combined with an appropriate image and feelings of familiarity and pastness, even though one did not remember the experience. This could happen if one's belief that one had had the experience arose from one's having been told about it. Such counter-examples could, however, be met by construing Russell's feelings of familiarity and pastness in such a way that they apply only to memory experiences. This would rather trivialize his analysis, but it is hard to see what other course is open.[38] The difficulty about personal identity remains unsolved, in any case, since if the analysis is not to be circular in this respect, it must leave open the possibility that the memory-belief is true of some experience which was not in fact one's own.

One of the most interesting features of Russell's account of memory is his introduction of what he calls "mnemic causation." The theory is that the past experience, in conjunction with some present stimulus, directly arouses the present memory, without the aid of any physiological intermediary to carry the traces of the experience. Russell argues that if we are looking upon causal laws as "*merely* observed uniformities of sequence," which is "all that science has to offer,"[39] we can have no logical objection to the idea of a causal connection in which one of the causal factors has ceased to exist. The only legitimate objection that we could have would be that this particular form of action at a distance appears to call for further explanation. However, in his book on *Human Knowledge*, which was

[38] See my *The Problem of Knowledge*, chap. iv.
[39] *The Analysis of Mind*, p. 89.

published twenty-seven years after *The Analysis of Mind*, Russell expresses dissatisfaction with "the view that causation is invariable sequence." He does not say what more exactly he thinks that it entails, but implies that he would at least reimpose the Humean condition that the cause be spatio-temporally contiguous with the effect. So mnemic causation is discarded, as being inconsistent with what Russell calls the postulate of spatio-temporal continuity. "We may," he now says, "recollect a given occurrence on various occasions, and in the intervening times there is nothing observable that belongs to the same causal line as the recollection, but we assume that there is *something* (in the brain?) which occurs at these intervening times, and makes the causal line continuous."[40]

C. HIS THEORY OF INDUCTION

Except in his book on *Human Knowledge*,[41] where he argues that even experiential propositions, as I have called them,[42] are open to doubt, Russell generally assumes that we can have certain knowledge of the character of the percepts, images, and feelings that occur within the specious present. On the other hand, the truth of any empirical proposition which goes at all beyond the immediate evidence is held by him to be uncertain. There are many such propositions about which we do not feel uncertain, but if we were being strictly logical we ought not, in Russell's opinion, to regard them as being more than highly probable. His reason for this is that, whether or not we are aware of making it, our belief in every such proposition is the

[40] *Human Knowledge*, p. 491.
[41] *Ibid.*, pp. 291 ff.
[42] See above, p. 76.

result of an inductive inference; and it is a feature of any inductive inference that its conclusion has a lesser degree of certainty than its premise.

This being his view, one might have expected Russell to pay more attention to the subject of induction than he actually does. He devotes a short chapter to it in *The Problems of Philosophy* but otherwise hardly mentions it at all until he finally attempts to deal with it fully in the last parts of his book on *Human Knowledge*. In *The Problems of Philosophy*, he remarks on the fallibility of "crude expectations of uniformity," such as those held by the chicken which expects the man who has fed it every day of its life to go on feeding it, whereas "he at last wrings its neck instead,"[43] but still agrees with Hume that it is only our discovery of past uniformities that can give us any good reason to believe either in any general law or in the occurrence of any future event. On this basis, he formulates the following "principle of induction," which he divides into two parts:

> (a) When a thing of a certain sort A has been found to be associated with a thing of a certain other sort B, and has never been found dissociated from a thing of the sort B, the greater the number of cases in which A and B have been associated, the greater is the probability that they will be associated in a fresh case in which one of them is known to be present; (b) Under the same circumstances, a sufficient number of cases of association will make the probability of a fresh association nearly a certainty, and will make it approach certainty without limit.[44]

Similarly, the principle lays it down that the probability of a general law, though less than that of a particular

[43] *The Problems of Philosophy*, p. 63.
[44] *Ibid.*, p. 66.

case, can also be increased by the repetition of favorable instances, and that it too can approach certainty without limit.

Russell says of this principle that it can be neither proved nor disproved by experience, but that "the general principles of science" as well as "the beliefs of daily life" are completely dependent on it.[45] This claim seems excessive, as the principle takes no account of the part that theories play in the development of science. Not many scientific hypotheses are straightforward generalizations from observed concomitances, though it could be argued that such generalizations emerge in the verification of more abstract laws. But the principle is anyhow insufficient, for a reason which Russell himself was later to give. The difficulty is that in any case in which A's and B's have been found to be uniformly associated, it will always be possible to find or devise another term B' which attributes the same property as B to the known instances of A but a property incompatible with B to the unknown instances. It will then follow, on Russell's principle, that however high the probability that the next A will be B, there is an equally high probability that it will not be B. Russell made this point, in a slightly different form, in the course of his discussion of probability in *Human Knowledge*. "Suppose," he says, "$a_1\ a_2\ \ldots\ a_n$ are members of a which have been observed and have been found to belong to a certain class β. Suppose that a_{n+1} is the next a to be observed. If it is a β, substitute for β the class consisting of β without a_{n+1}. For this class the induction breaks down. This sort of argument is obviously capable of extension. It follows that if induction is to have any chance of validity, a and β must not be *any* classes, but classes having certain properties or re-

[45] *Ibid.*, p. 69.

lations."[46] It is the selection of these favored classes that constitutes what Nelson Goodman has called the new riddle of induction.[47] One thing that is obvious is that no single principle of uniformity will do this work, just because it will be too general.

As the passage which I have just cited shows, Russell's treatment of the problem in *Human Knowledge* is both more subtle and more cautious. He distinguishes two different concepts which he regards as having an equal claim, on the basis of usage, to the title of probability. One of them is "mathematical probability, which is numerically measurable and satisfies the axioms of the probability calculus":[48] this is the concept which is used in statistics and in games of chance. The other is one to which Russell gives the name of "degree of credibility." This applies to every empirical proposition, and is based upon the relevant evidence, whether the evidence consists of other propositions, which themselves will have some degree of credibility, or whether, as in the case of experiential propositions, it consists in the actual occurrence of some experience. "In some cases," Russell says, "the degree of credibility can be inferred from mathematical probability, in others it cannot; but even when it can it is important to remark that it is a different concept. It is this sort, and not mathematical probability, that is relevant when it is said that all our knowledge is only probable, and that probability is the guide of life."[49]

After examining various analyses of the concept of mathematical probability, Russell concludes that the best course is to equate probability, in this sense, with

[46] *Human Knowledge*, pp. 413–14.
[47] See Nelson Goodman, *Fact, Fiction and Forecast*, chap. III.
[48] *Human Knowledge*, p. 343.
[49] *Ibid.*, p. 344.

the frequency with which a property is distributed among the members of some finite class. Thus, to say that the probability of throwing double six with a pair of dice is 1/36 is to say that the combination of 6 and 6 is one out of 36 possible results, or else, perhaps, that in the actual series of throws which are made with the dice the combination of 6 and 6 occurs once in 36 times. These two interpretations are not equivalent, and it is a defect in Russell's exposition that it does not distinguish between the cases in which the membership of a class is determined logically and those in which it is determined empirically. The reason for this, no doubt, is that he is mainly interested in statistical judgments, to which his analysis applies unambiguously. Thus, to say that there was a probability m/n that a child born in London in the year 1850 would attain the age of eighty is, on this view, just to say that a proportion m/n of the children born in London in that year did attain that age.

An advantage of this interpretation is that judgments of probability are given a definite truth-value. There must always be one definite ratio in which a given property occurs among the members of a given finite class, and the judgment of probability will be true if it specifies this ratio and false if it does not. The trouble is, however, that this ratio will usually not be ascertainable. Not only are we seldom in a position to examine all the members of a class, but in most cases we do not even know what this totality is. We are assuming that the class is finite but we do not know how far its membership extends. In these circumstances, we do not have much hope of making a judgment of probability which will be exactly true. We shall be satisfied if our assessment of the ratio is approximately correct. If in going through the members of a class we come to a point where the incidence of a property P remains fixed in the neighborhood of m/n, we conjecture that m/n is approximately the ratio in which P is distributed through-out the whole class. But what justification have we for making this conjecture, if we do not know the extension of the class? At this point it is customary to invoke the law of large numbers, which gives us the mathematical assurance that as the size of our sample increases, it becomes increasingly probable that the incidence of a property in the sample matches its incidence in the parent class from which the sample is drawn. But all that this comes to is that in relation to all possible samples of a given size, the number of those in which the inci-dence of some property deviates from its incidence in the parent class is relatively small, and becomes smaller as the size of the sample increases. But then, in default of some postulate of fair sampling, what right have we to assume that our actual samples are not deviant? This is a problem which Russell appears to overlook.

An important point which Russell does notice is that mathematical probability does not apply to individual cases. A judgment of probability of this sort, which appears to be about an individual, has always to be con-strued as a judgment about some class to which the individual belongs. Not only that, but when we do try to apply it to an individual, we get contradictory results, according as the individual is assigned to different classes. Thus, the probability, in this sense, that I shall live to the age of eighty will almost certainly be differ-ent, according as I am regarded as a member of the class of Englishmen in general, or of Englishmen born in the first quarter of this century, or British philoso-phers, or philosophers in general, or heavy cigarette-smokers, or moderate drinkers, or fellows of an Oxford college, or persons whose surname begins with A, or any combination of these classes, or any other of the vast number of classes to which I belong. So far as mathematical probability goes, there is nothing to choose between any of these conflicting judgments. Whether the class to which they refer be that of heavy cigarette-smokers or persons whose surname begins with A, the most that can be asked is that they get the ratio right. If, nevertheless, my membership of the former class is regarded as having more bearing on my chances of longevity than my membership of the latter, this is because the judgment about my chances is construed as a judgment of degree of credibility, in relation to which the ratios which obtain in the various classes to which I happen to belong are not of equal weight. When we come to judgments of this kind, we look for causal factors, and in the cases where we are not able to subsume the event in which we are interested under what we take to be a causal law, we relate it to the strongest statement of tendency which we believe to be extrapolable. But what constitutes a strong statement of tendency, and under what conditions such statements are extrapolable, are difficult questions into which Russell does not enter.

The problem which chiefly concerns him, with regard to judgments of degree of credibility, is how to secure a high probability, in this sense, for statements of law. He relies on a theorem of Keynes's, according to which a sufficiently long run of exclusively favorable instances bestows on a generalization a probability tending to certainty as a limit, provided that the generalization has some initial probability, antecedently to the observation of any of its instances, and provided that if the generalization is false, the probability that we should come across only favorable instances of it tends to zero as the number of those instances increases.[50] As a theorem in mathematical probability, this is a variant of the law of large numbers. If one assumes, as Russell does, that the class of A's is finite, then the proviso that the

[50] *Ibid.*, p. 435.

generalization "All A's are B" should have some initial probability can be held to be satisfied by the fact that all the A's being B, as opposed to this or that fraction of them, is one of a finite number of logical possibilities. Similarly, the second condition is satisfied by the fact that if not all A's are B, then as the size of our samples increases, there will be a decreasing proportion, among all possible samples of a given size, of those which contain no A that is not B. When interpreted in this way the theorem is valid, but again we need to introduce a postulate of fair sampling if we are to draw any inferences from it as to what is actually the case. Russell, however, like Keynes, makes a tacit and unwarranted shift from mathematical probability to degree of credibility. He thinks it necessary to show that some generalizations at least have an initial degree of credibility, and realizing that it would be circular to attempt to derive this from their resemblance to other generalizations which are inductively established, he looks for some general principles which will bestow an initial degree of credibility on certain types of generalizations, and thereby provide a justification for our inductive reasoning.

The principles which Russell devises for this purpose are five in number and are called by him, respectively, the postulate of quasi-permanence, the postulate of separable causal lines, the postulate of spatio-temporal continuity in causal lines, the structural postulate, and the postulate of analogy.[51] The postulate of quasi-permanence is that "Given any event A, it happens very frequently that, at any neighbouring time, there is at some neighbouring place an event very similar to A."[52] The function of this postulate is to provide for the

[51] *Ibid.*, p. 487.
[52] *Ibid.*, p. 488.

existence of material continuants. It relies on the assumption that even if two states of the same thing, which are widely separated in time, may be qualitatively very different, as, for example, a person in infancy may bear very little resemblance to the same person as an old man, the process of change is usually very gradual. This can also be seen as a reductive postulate, securing the replacement of things by events.

The postulate of separable causal lines is that "it is frequently possible to form a series of events such that from one or two members of the series something can be inferred as to all the other members."[53] Russell explains that this postulate is primarily intended to cover the laws of motion. It too is a reductive postulate, in that it replaces the concept of a thing's changing its position by that of a suitably related series of events.

The postulate of spatio-temporal continuity is designed to eliminate action at a distance. It applies only to series of events which are taken to constitute separable causal lines and entails that the causality within these series is continuous. There seems to be no particular reason for this postulate except that it reflects a common scientific preference.

The postulate of structure is needed for Russell's theory of perception. It is that "When a number of structurally similar complex events are ranged about a centre in regions not widely separated, it is usually the case that all belong to causal lines having their origin in an event of the same structure at the centre."[54] What is meant by the events' being ranged about a center is illustrated by the case in which an object is simultaneously seen or photographed from a number of different positions. "The visual percepts and the photographs can

---

[53] *Ibid.*, p. 489.
[54] *Ibid.*, p. 492.

be arranged by the laws of perspective, and by the same laws the position of the object seen and photographed can be determined."[55] This postulate also allows us to infer a common cause in such cases as the existence of different copies of the same book or different receptions of the same wireless program.

Finally, the postulate of analogy is chiefly intended to deal with a problem to which Russell otherwise devotes little attention: that of one's knowledge of the existence and functioning of minds other than one's own. The postulate is that "Given two classes of events A and B, and given that, whenever both A and B can be observed, there is reason to believe that A causes B, then if, in a given case, A is observed, but there is no way of observing whether B occurs or not, it is probable that B occurs: and similarly, if B is observed, but the presence or absence of A cannot be observed."[56] Russell remarks that this postulate, besides affording us a reason for believing in the mental states of others, also enables us to make such inferences as that bodies which have given us the sensation of hardness remain hard when they are not being touched. He does not deal with the objection, which some philosophers have raised, that there is a significant difference in these arguments from analogy, in that the association of visual with tactile data is something that I have frequently observed and am able to test, whereas I have never observed, nor can I directly test, the association of a bodily state of another person with the mental state which is supposed to be causally related to it. In this respect, our belief in the mental life of others is assimilable to our belief in the existence of the past, where again there is no possibility of our actually comparing

[55] *Ibid.*
[56] *Ibid.*, p. 413.

our present recollections with the past events for which we take them to be evidence.

Russell says that there can be no question of proving his five postulates. He does not claim that they are analytically true, and he thinks that any attempt to establish them inductively will be circular, since all our inductive reasoning presupposes them. It seems to me, however, that if our inductive reasoning does presuppose them, it is not quite in the way that Russell suggests. Whatever other purposes they may serve, I do not see how they could be used to license the special inductive inferences that we wish to make. They are much too general to be of any help in solving the new riddle of induction.[57] They do not instruct us which properties to project. If they can nevertheless be regarded as pre-suppositions of scientific method, it is because they may be taken as descriptions of what Quine has called the background theory,[58] in terms of which we interpret our experiences. At any rate they draw the main outlines of Russell's own version of this theory. They set out the framework of his picture of reality.

[57] See above, p. 95
[58] See W. V. Quine, *Ontological Relativity*, pp. 51 ff.

Russell's Conception of Reality

IV

In the account of his philosophy which he con-
tributed to the first volume of *Contemporary
British Philosophy* in 1924, Russell chose to describe his philosophical standpoint as that of
Logical Atomism. Though we shall see that he
modified it in certain respects, the world view
which he summarized under this heading is one
that he substantially continued to hold throughout the remainder of his career.

The basic thesis of logical atomism, as he
presented it in this essay[1] and in the series of
lectures on "The Philosophy of Logical Atomism," which he delievered six years previously,
was that the world consists of simple particulars
which have only simple qualities and stand only

[1] Reprinted in *Logic and Knowledge* under the title
"Logical Atomism."

in simple relations to one another. This does not pre-
clude their being credited with complex properties, but
these must then be analyzable into simple ones. It is left
open whether the number of these particulars is finite
or infinite. Both qualities and relations are external to
their subjects, in the sense that neither singly nor in
combination are they essential to the subject's identity:
in theory, it could have a wholly different set of properties and still be the same particular. This is not inconsistent with its being identifiable only through its properties, since an object can be identified by any feature
which in fact distinguishes it from other objects, for
example its spatio=temporal position, without its possession of this feature being necessary for it to be the object that it is.

Simple objects, for Russell, are those that can be
denoted by logically proper names. And since it follows
from his theory of descriptions that any nominative
expression, which is not a proper name, can be analyzed
into predicates, this already entails that all genuine
objects must be simple. It follows also that the question
whether an object is simple or complex, or, to speak
more accurately, whether it is a genuine object or what
Russell calls a logical fiction, depends entirely on the
question what properties are ascribable to it. In short,
the simplicity and therefore genuineness of an object is
measured by the simplicity of its qualities.

Russell gives no criterion for the simplicity of qualities, but if I am right in what I have said about the
bearers of logically proper names,[2] it would seem that
these qualities must be absolutely specific, homogene-
ous, and directly exemplified within our experience.
These conditions are satisfied by the qualities of percepts. The question, however, becomes more difficult in

[2] See above, p. 53.

Russell's later works when he admits objects which are not given in experience. What can the simple qualities of such objects be? The only answer which seems available to Russell is that they are qualities which have some structural similarity to the qualities of percepts and are also sufficient to cause them.

Another formal difficulty is that these external objects, being known to us only by description, cannot be denoted by logically proper names, but this is less serious, since we have seen that the tendency of the theory of descriptions is to show that names can be dispensed with. Russell himself does not explicitly draw this conclusion but, as we shall see in a moment, he draws it implicitly, when, in *An Inquiry into Meaning and Truth* and thereafter, he makes names stand for complexes of qualities. For this means that although he may continue to speak of the use of names, he is in fact ceasing to employ them, in the sense in which he first conceived of them. The proof of this is that a name, in this new sense, may be significant even though the complex of qualities which it purports to name does not exist.

The discarding of names goes together with the elimination of particulars. The question whether there is, as he put it, "an ultimate dualism" between particulars and universals, which he took to be equivalent to the question whether subject-predicate propositions can be "analysed into propositions of other forms, which do not require a radical difference of nature between the apparent subject and the apparent predicate"[3] is one to which Russell gives different answers at different times. One point on which he is consistent is in not thinking it possible to dispense with universals by replacing expres-

[3] "On the Relation of Universals and Particulars," in *Logic and Knowledge*, p. 109.

ties,"[7] on the ground that whatever qualities are possessed by such a subject, it is logically possible that some other subject should have them as well.

So far as I can see, this argument is simply equivalent to a denial of the identity of indiscernibles, the principle that there cannot logically be two different things which have all their properties in common. As such it may be acceptable, but even so it is not enough to establish that there are particulars, in the sense that Russell intended. I cannot make up my mind whether the principle of the identity of indiscernibles is true or false, but the considerations which tend to make me think it false, such as the apparent intelligibility of fantasies like that of there being another universe which mirrors this one, or the Nietzschean idea of eternal recurrence, are all such as to favor, not the introduction of substances, as entities distinct from their attributes, but rather the admission of the possibility that things which cannot be descriptively distinguished may still be distinguished demonstratively. This ties in with the theory of descriptions, where we have seen that, on the assumption that variables can be explained away, it is only in the possible need for demonstratives that an echo of particulars is retained.

Many years later, Russell himself came to accept the identity of indiscernibles and so to believe in the possibility of eliminating particulars. In *An Inquiry into Meaning and Truth*, and more fully in *Human Knowledge*, he attempts to show that they can be replaced by complexes of qualities. For this purpose, he introduces the undefined relation of "compresence" which holds between qualities which occur at the same time in the same total experience. Thus, all my present visual, auditory, and tactual data, as well as any images or feelings

[7] *Ibid.*, p. 120.

that I may be having, are mutually compresent. "I thus arrive," Russell says, "at a group having the two properties: (a) that all the members of the group are compresent, (b) that nothing outside the group is compresent with every member of the group. Such a group I shall call a 'complete complex of compresence.' "[8]

There are two serious defects in this account, which have to be remedied if complete complexes of compresence are to do the work that Russell requires of them. In the first place, if they are going to replace physical objects, they cannot be limited to qualities which fall within some total experience. The only physical objects of which Russell thinks that we have direct experience are our own brains, and he certainly does not wish to imply that these are the only physical objects that there are. The reference to a total experience must therefore be taken to be purely illustrative: it draws our attention to the only instances of compresence of which we can have any first-hand knowledge. In its application to qualities outside our experience, the relation of compresence is clearly intended to be one of spatio-temporal coincidence, but it cannot be defined as such, since it is itself used to define the terms which are used in the construction of our spatio-temporal system.

The second defect in Russell's account is that the properties which he assigns to a complete complex of compresence are not sufficient for his purpose. It has to be remembered that he is dealing with qualities and that for two qualities to be compresent it is sufficient that they occur together on any one occasion. But then it may well happen that a quality which one would wish to exclude from the group, as not being a property at the relevant time of the "thing" which the group was

[8] *Human Knowledge*, p. 294.

meant to constitute, was nevertheless compresent with every member of the group; the reason for not including it would be that it was not compresent with them all at once. Russell cannot meet this difficulty by applying the relation of compresence to the instances of his qualities, since the qualities have no instances. The occasions of their manifestation, which would ordinarily be described as their instances, have themselves to be constructed out of the uniqueness of the complexes in which the qualities participate. The solution is rather to strengthen the second clause in his definition. To the proviso that no quality outside the group is compresent with every member of it, we need to add the proviso that no quality outside the group is compresent with every complex quality which is constituted by the compresence of members of the group. On the assumption of the identity of indiscernibles, this will give us what we need.

What it will not give us is a unique specification of an instance of the set of qualities in question, since it remains logically possible that a complete complex should be duplicated both in space and time. Russell admits this possibility and consequently also admits that, on his interpretation of them, such propositions as that the same thing cannot occupy two different places at the same time, or that if A wholly precedes B, A and B are not identical, are not necessarily true. The first of these propositions would be falsified if a complete complex of compresence were simultaneously duplicated in space, and the second if it were duplicated in time, since it would in that case precede itself. Nevertheless he thinks it reasonably safe to assume that such propositions are contingently true, since he considers it improbable that any complete complex of compresence is actually duplicated. The main reason which he gives for thinking this improbable is that the complexes contain memory experiences, which are very unlikely to be exactly the same on two different occasions.

Here Russell again forgets that his complete complexes of compresence also have to constitute physical objects, to which he does not wish to attribute the exercise of memory. And while he does not credit us with any knowledge of the intrinsic qualities of physical objects, he has no good reason to assume that their total momentary states are never duplicated. It might, indeed, be argued that since they are known to us only by description as the postulated causes of our experiences, the uniqueness of their qualities at any given place and time is secured by the uniqueness of the total experiences to the ingredients of which they are causally related. But the answer to this is that our conception of the physical world is not limited to those objects that cause our actual percepts: it also includes the hypothetical causes of sensibilia, or merely possible percepts, and we have no right to assume that complete complexes of sensibilia are not duplicated.

The consequence is that to obtain individuation, we may be obliged in certain cases to identify an object not by its qualities but by its environment, and this might seem to be a lapse from Russell's principle of atomicity. The lapse is, however, not very serious. If, as seems best, we individuate them by reference to landmarks, which may either be real complexes that we can confidently assume not to be duplicated, or else, as in our actual dating system, fictitious complexes which are postulated as being unique, or a combination of the two, our atomic objects will indeed suffer some loss of logical independence, to the extent that they are identified by reference to one another. Nevertheless the relations of the object to actual landmarks, or their relations to one another, which fix their relations to the fictitious landmarks, will in all cases be contingent: and since the choice of landmarks will be arbitrary, in the sense that it will be dictated only by convenience, it will follow that even in the cases where our reference to an object does imply the existence of something else, there will still be no two objects of which it will be necessarily true that referring to either implies the existence of the other. Consequently, the principle of atomicity is not seriously violated.

It may also be objected that if objects are to be turned into complexes of qualities they will cease to be atomic: but this again is not a serious difficulty. It is true, as Russell says in *An Inquiry into Meaning and Truth*, that if "W" names a complex of qualities, and the complex is defined by the enumeration of its members, then the proposition that a quality q is a member of W will, if true, be analytic: but this proves only that "W" is not what Russell would previously have regarded as a genuine name. The important point is that the relation of compresence which unites the members of W is itself contingent. It is now the qualities that are the basic elements of the system, and the principle of atomicity is secured by the assumption that they are simple.

B. MIND AND MATTER

"That the world contains facts, which are what they are whatever we may choose to think about them" is said by Russell to be an obvious truism.[9] This statement occurs in the first of his lectures on The Philosophy of Logical Atomism, which, as we have seen, owed much to Wittgenstein, and his reason for making it was presumably the same as that which led Wittgenstein to begin his *Tractatus Logico-Philosophicus* with the prop-

---

[9] *Logic and Knowledge*, p. 182.

ositions that "The world is everything that is the case.
The world is the totality of facts, not of things."[10] They
both assumed a correspondence between the structure
of language and the structure of the world, which meant
that facts were needed to give propositions, or sentences,
something to reflect. Atomic facts are what make atomic
propositions true.

At a later stage, when he is less under the influence
of the pictorial view of language, Russell tends to replace
facts by events. He continues to speak of there being
facts as states of affairs which make propositions true or
false, independently of our beliefs, but generally appears
to hold that these states of affairs are better described
as events. This is not to say that he chooses to use the
word "event" as a synonym for "fact" but rather that
everything that one might want to say about empirical
facts can be more informatively rephrased as a statement about events. In his latest work he often writes as if
with events he had reached "the ultimate furniture of the
world," but in fact he believes that events themselves
are analyzable into qualities. An event consists in the
location of a group of qualities in some small region of
space-time, the regions of space-time being themselves
constructed, as we have seen, out of relations between
groups of qualities. It will, however, be simpler to follow Russell's example in continuing to speak of events.
In that case, we shall not also need to speak of things,
in the sense of physical or mental continuants, since
they can be identified with series of events which are
suitably interrelated by spatio-temporal contiguity and
by their fulfillment of certain causal laws.

What then can be said about the character of the
events which constitute the world? An opinion which

[10] Ludwig Wittgenstein, *Tractatus Logico-Philosophicus*, 1.
and 1.1.

has been widely held, both before and after it was given the authority of Descartes, is that objects or events are divisible into the two classes of mental and physical, which do not overlap; but this is a view which Russell consistently contests. Thus in *The Analysis of Mind* he asserts that "The stuff of which the world of our experience is composed is, in my belief, neither mind nor matter, but something more primitive than either."[11] This neutral stuff, as we have seen, was thought by him to consist in sensibilia which enter into the constitution of both minds and bodies, together with images and feelings which enter only into the constitution of minds. To the extent that minds and bodies consisted of common elements, they were differentiated by the participation of these elements in different groups, conforming to different causal laws. A problem, however, arises when Russell gives up this position, which has come to be known as that of neutral monism, in favor of one in which physical objects are represented as inferred entities, rather than as logical constructions. He repeatedly says that we can know nothing about the intrinsic qualities of these external objects or of the events to which they are reducible, so that it remains theoretically possible that they have the qualities which we know to characterize our percepts. At the same time, he maintains that we have no good reason to believe that they do have anything more than a purely structural resemblance to percepts and, in the light of our knowledge of the causal conditions of perception, some good reason to believe that they do not.

Since this view appears to put the occurrence of percepts into the category of what would ordinarily be counted as mental events, as opposed to the unknown physical events which are postulated as their causes, it

[11] *The Analysis of Mind*, p. 10.

is rather surprising that Russell continues to maintain that the distinction between the mental and the physical is not a distinction in the nature of events. Thus in an essay on "Mind and Matter" which was published as late as 1958, in the collection entitled *Portraits from Memory*, he says that "An event is not rendered either mental or material by any intrinsic quality, but only by its causal relations. It is perfectly possible for an event to have both the causal relations characteristic of physics and those characteristic of psychology. In that case, the event is both mental and material at once."[12] This contradicts his earlier view that images and feelings are intrinsically mental, in the sense that it is because of their qualities and not just their relations that they enter only into the constitution of minds. The change comes about because he has come to hold that mental events are not merely located in the brain, but are identical with states of the brain. "The events," he says, "that are grouped to make a given mind are, according to my theory, the very same events that are grouped to make its brain. Or perhaps it would be more correct to say that they are *some* of the events that make the brain. The important point is, that the difference between mind and brain is not a difference of quality, but a difference of arrangement."[13]

The question then arises whether the events which are common to mind and brain have the known qualities of percepts, images, and feelings, or the unknown qualities of physical events, or both. The first answer is suggested by Russell's saying that "the brain consists of thoughts—using 'thought' in its widest sense, as it was used by Descartes,"[14] but this is hard to reconcile with

[12] *Portraits from Memory*, p. 152 (Readers Union Edition p. 159).
[13] *Ibid.*, p. 148 (Readers Union Edition p. 154).
[14] *My Philosophical Development*, p. 25.

his saying that we have no good reason to believe that the physical events, which cause our experiences, are qualitatively similar to the experiences which they cause. Equally, the second answer is hard to reconcile with Russell's view that what I have called experiential propositions, the expressions of our judgments about the contents of our current experiences, come as near to being certain as any empirical propositions can. As for the third answer, I do not see how it can well be true that one and the same occurrence can both, *qua* mental event, have the quality, say, of a mental image, and, *qua* physical event, have qualities which do no more than structually correspond with the qualities of anything that actually enters into an experience. I have to confess, therefore, that I am unable to make sense of Russell's position on this point.

Russell's picture of the world, of which this identification of mind and brain, and the conception of physical events as having a structural correspondence to the percepts which they cause, are the most important features, is intended to be in harmony with contemporary scientific theories. "Science," says Russell, "is at no moment quite right, but it is seldom quite wrong, and has, as a rule, a better chance of being right than the theories of the unscientific. It is, therefore, rational to accept it hypothetically."[15] I entirely agree with this conclusion, but do not believe, any more, indeed, than Russell himself did, that the general account of reality which he develops in his later work is the only one consistent with it. For reasons which I have given in discussing his theory of perception, I think that the simpler method, which I there outlined,[16] of blending a form of scientific realism with a form of neutral monism is philosophically more acceptable.

[15] *Ibid.*, p. 17.
[16] See above, p. 85–86.

Russell's Moral Philosophy

A. ETHICS

While it was obvious to anyone who knew him, and is also apparent from his extensive writings on social and political questions, that Russell held very strong moral convictions, he devoted comparatively little attention to ethical theory. His contribution to the pure, as opposed to the applied, philosophy of morals is almost wholly contained in two of his published works; one of them an essay on "The Elements of Ethics" which he brought out in installments, chiefly in the year 1910, and reprinted in his *Philosophical Essays*, and the other his book on *Human Society in Ethics and Politics*, of which the ethical part was mainly written in 1945–1946, although the book was not published until 1954.

In "The Elements of Ethics," Russell defends a position which is closely modeled, as he acknowledges, on that which his friend G. E. Moore had adopted in his *Principia Ethica*. In particular, he follows Moore in treating good as an indefinable non-natural quality, in holding that the question whether and to what degree some state of affairs is intrinsically good has an objectively true answer, which is discoverable only by intuition, and in defining an objectively right action as the one, out of all the actions open to the agent, that would have the best consequences, in the sense that it would result in the greatest preponderance of good or, in the case where no favorable balance of good is attainable, the smallest preponderance of evil.

In the elaboration of these propositions, Russell is chiefly concerned with the question of right conduct. He sees that it would not be sensible to require people to do what is objectively right, according to his definition, since they are not able to foresee the total consequences of their actions, let alone calculate all the hypothetical consequences of the actions that they could have performed instead. The most that can be asked is that they perform the action that will probably have the best consequences, in the light of whatever information they possess, or can reasonably be expected to collect. Russell speaks of an action which satisfies this condition as the wisest possible action and equates it with that which it is right for the agent to do.

It is clear that the right action, in this sense, is not necessarily identical with what Russell calls the most fortunate or objectively right action. Neither is it necessarily identical with what Russell calls the subjectively right action, which is what the agent believes to be right. One reason why it may not be is that the agent may make a false judgment of probability, and another is that he may hold a different moral theory. He may act in accordance with some moral principle which he believes to be binding on him, even though he does not think it probable that his action will have the best con-

sequences. He may even think the consequences irrelevant: "Let justice be done though the heavens fall."
Russell is disturbed by cases of this kind, because he is
inclined to hold that a man ought to do what his conscience tells him to. His conscience may not be enlightened, he may be burdened with a set of superstitious
principles which have lost what utility they ever may
have had. Even so, can we say that he has acted morally,
if he has done anything other than what he sincerely
believes to be right? Russell does not think that we can,
and consequently defines a moral action as one that the
agent would judge to be right "after an appropriate
amount of candid thought,"[17] this condition being
added to provide for the case where the agent mistakes
some other motive for the voice of conscience, or hastily
overlooks considerations which would have led him to
judge differently if he had taken them into account.

A point which escapes Russell's notice is that in his
account of what constitutes a moral action, he uses the
word "right" in a different sense from that in which he
has defined it. If he adhered to his own definition, he
would have to mean that an action was moral when the
agent candidly judged it to be likely to have the best
consequences. That he does not mean this is clear from
the fact, which we have already noted, that one of his
reasons for distinguishing between a right and a moral
action is that people sometimes judge actions to be right
irrespectively of their consequences. The explanation of
this inconsistency is that his definition of "right" is not
intended to state what is ordinarily meant by the word.
It is rather what is now known as a persuasive definition,
its object being to annex to the idea of doing what will
probably have the best consequences the feelings that
we already have about doing what is right. If this enter-

[17] *Philosophical Essays*, p. 36.

prise were successful, so that it came to be generally agreed that the only thing to be taken into account in estimating the rightness of an action was its probable consequences, the persuasive definition might then pass muster as a definition of the ordinary sort. Even so, the point that the moral use of words like "right" and "good" is primarily normative rather than descriptive would still remain valid.

The ruling that we are to choose from among all possible actions the one that will probably have the best consequences brings up the question what actions are possible. Is it in fact ever possible for a man to do anything but what he actually does? A believer in determinism might argue that it was not, and consequently that we have only the illusion of choice. Conversely, one who believes that we really can choose how to act, in a sense which makes us morally responsible for what we choose, might use this as an argument against determinism and in favor of the existence of free will. Russell, who considers the question at some length, disagrees with both these positions. He thinks that determinism is very likely to be true, but does not think that its truth would entail that no actions except those that were actually performed could correctly be said to have been possible. He holds it sufficient to make an action possible that it should be physically within the agent's power, in the sense that he would do it if he willed to. Like Locke, whom he follows on this point, Russell is not troubled by the question whether, and if so in what sense, it is possible for us to will anything other than we do. It is enough that our actions should be causally dependent on our choices, no matter how these may be caused.

There are many who would say that we need to be free in a stronger sense than this, if we are to be morally responsible. But Russell's answer to this is that if what they mean by our having free will is that the operations of our wills should be uncaused, then, so far from its being the case that the attribution of moral responsibility presupposes the existence of free will, the two are incompatible.

> If we really believed that other people's actions did not have causes, we could never try to influence other people's actions: for such influence can only result if we know, more or less, what causes will produce the actions we desire. If we could never try to influence other people's actions . . . argument, exhortation, and command would become mere idle breath. Thus almost all the actions with which morality is concerned would become irrational . . . and right and wrong would be interfered with in a way in which determinism certainly does not interfere with them. Most morality absolutely depends upon the assumption that volitions have causes, and nothing in morals is destroyed by this assumption.[18]

In this argument, Russell, in my view rightly, treats motives as causes. He does not discuss the forlorn attempt, which some philosophers have made, to salvage free will by distinguishing between acting for a reason and acting from a cause. He does, however, see that his adherence to determinism creates a problem about the justification for praise or blame. If a man's choices are determined, how can he be held accountable for making them? Russell's answer, which goes back to Hume, is that the only justification for praise or blame, reward or punishment, is that we expect to influence future choices. By inflicting pain on a man who has performed a socially harmful action, we hope to deter him from repeating it and to deter others by the example. What is not justifiable is any retributive idea of punishment.

[18] *Philosophical Essays*, pp. 43–44.

I think that this is the correct conclusion to be drawn from Russell's premises, and am also of the opinion that the notion of our deserving reward or punishment cannot be rationally upheld.[19] At the same time, I think that Russell underrates the extent to which this position conflicts with our ordinary moral outlook. We do hold that people are morally responsible for their actions, in a sense which implies that they ought to benefit or suffer on their account, though not perhaps in equal measure. Inconsistently, we are more inclined to let virtue be its own reward than vice its own retribution. Russell himself acknowledges this feeling in a passage where he admits that "When I am compelled, as happens very frequently in the modern world, to contemplate acts of cruelty which make me shudder with horror, I find myself constantly impelled towards an ethical outlook which I cannot justify intellectually."[20] He resists this impulse by reasoning that "It does not follow, because A is cruel, that B is right to be cruel towards A. It follows only that he does right in trying to prevent A from committing further cruel acts. If, as may well happen, this is more likely to be effected by kindness than by punishment, then kindness is the better method."[21] This reasoning is surely sound, but it is not always emotionally easy to accept.

In his book on *Human Society in Ethics and Politics*, Russell maintains his position on free will, together with the view that the rightness of an action is decided by its probable consequences, but gives up the remainder of his earlier theory. He says that there is no logical objection to the theory that we know by ethical intuition what kinds of actions we ought to perform, but that

[19] See my essay on "Man as a Subject for Science," in *Metaphysics and Common Sense*.
[20] *Human Society in Ethics and Politics*, p. 128.
[21] *Ibid.*, pp. 128–29.

it has "a great drawback, namely, that there is no general agreement as to what sorts of acts ought to be performed, and that the theory affords no means of deciding who is in the right where there is disagreement. It thus becomes, in practice though not in theory, an egocentric doctrine." With each party claiming an intuition of the truth, "ethical controversy will become merely a clash of rival dogmas."[22] This objection does not apply so strongly to the theory that we can know by intuition what is good, in the sense of possessing intrinsic value, since this is a matter on which there are fewer serious disagreements. Nevertheless, he thinks that there are enough for the objection still to hold. Moreover, the fact that the things to which we are inclined to attach intrinsic value are all things which are desired or enjoyed suggests to him that good, in this sense, "may be definable in terms of desire or pleasure or both."[23]

Russell briefly considers some other theories which seem to him untenable. His objection to the theory that morals can be grounded on divine authority is contained in one sentence: "Theologians have always taught that God's decrees are good, and that this is not a mere tautology; it follows that goodness is logically independent of God's decrees."[24] This is beautifully succinct and quite decisive. His objection to egoism, the doctrine that one should aim only to maximize one's own pleasure, is that it rests on the assumption that one can have no other aim, and that this is psychologically false. "What is true," he says, "in psychological hedonism is that *my* desires inevitably determine *my* behaviour. What is false is (1) that my desires are always for my pleasure, (2) that my desires are limited to what is going

[22] *Ibid.*, p. 111.
[23] *Ibid.*, p. 113.
[24] *Ibid.*, p. 48.

to happen to me."[25] This argument is not new, but the critical part of it is obviously correct. It is not perhaps so obvious that all one's behavior is determined by desire, but if we restrict its application to purposive as opposed to merely habitual behavior, and at the same time extend the notion of desire so that it covers any motive, the proposition may pass for being analytic: and in fact this appears to be the way in which Russell interprets it.

At this period, Russell attaches less importance to the claims of conscience than he did in his earlier work. He tends rather to make fun of its vagaries. "The Dukhobors refused military service, but held it proper to dance naked all together round a camp fire; being persecuted for the former tenet in Russia, they emigrated to Canada, where they were persecuted for the latter. The Mormons had a divine revelation in favour of polygamy, but under pressure from the United States government they discovered that the revelation was not binding. Some moralists, including many eminent Jesuits, have considered tyrannicide a duty; others have taught that it is always a sin."[26] The moral is that there has to be some other criterion by which to test the deliverances of conscience, which too often merely reflect the uncritical acceptance of wholly irrational taboos. This is factually correct, but the difficulty of expecting a man to act otherwise than as his conscience bids him still remains.

Russell is critical also of the Kantian and Stoic view that virtue is an end in itself, especially in the Kantian version of it, where virtue is confined to obeying the moral law for its own sake. "If you are kind to your brother because you are fond of him, you have no merit; but if you can hardly stand him and are nevertheless kind to him because the moral law says you should be,

25 *Ibid.*, p. 64.
26 *Ibid.*, p. 46.

then you are the sort of person that Kant thinks you ought to be."[27] He thinks it inconsistent of Kant to have argued in favor of an afterlife, on the ground of its being unjust that the good should suffer without any future recompense, remarking that if Kant "really believed what he thinks he believes, he would not regard heaven as a place where the good are happy, but as a place where they have never-ending opportunities of doing kindnesses to people whom they dislike."[28] This is unfair to Kant, who was mainly actuated by the admittedly false belief that freedom of action, which he thought that morality presupposed, was to be found only in obedience to the moral law, but one can sympathize with Russell's antipathy to a stern morality of duty, in which the concern for human happiness, at any rate in this life, plays no part.

Russell's own theory is very similar to that of Hume. As I said earlier,[29] he starts with Hume's dictum that "reason is, and ought only to be, the slave of the passions."[30] This is not an uncharacteristic concession to irrationalism, but just a rhetorical way of making the point that the ends of our actions are determined by our desires: the role of reason is only to ensure a choice of the proper means. If, as does sometimes happen, we speak of ends themselves as rational or irrational, we are either employing a misleading way of expressing our approval or disapproval of them, or else we are treating them as means: thus, we may say that an end is irrational if it conflicts with other ends to which we attach greater importance.

If nothing can be an end unless it is desired, the

[27] *Ibid.*, p. 49.
[28] *Ibid.*
[29] See above, p. 27.
[30] David Hume, *A Treatise of Human Nature*, Book II, Part III, Section III.

things at which we are encouraged to aim must be things that we are capable of desiring. It is for this reason, no doubt, that Russell says that "ethics differs from science in the fact that its fundamental data are feelings and emotions, not percepts."[31] At the same time, he assimilates it to science by making it descriptive, while displaying some uncertainty as to what it describes. Thus at one point he says that there are various possible definitions of "good," but that the one of which the "consequences will be found more consonant with the ethical feelings of the majority of mankind" is that "an occurrence is 'good' when it satisfies desire."[32] At another point, having said that actions are judged in terms of their probable effects, he goes on to say that "effects which lead to approval are defined as 'good' and those leading to disapproval as 'bad.' "[33] I suppose that these definitions are to be reconciled by making the assumption that the effects which lead to approval are those which are thought likely to satisfy desire. The question then arises whether in calling something good, I am saying just that I approve of it, or that it is an object of general approval, either among the members of my society, or among mankind at large. If I am saying that it is an object of general approval, the implication will be that it is generally thought desirable: but if I am saying only that I approve of it, this could be either on the ground of its satisfying my own desire, or on the ground of its giving general satisfaction.

Russell does not distinguish at all clearly between these different possibilities, but in the main he appears to hold that in calling something good I am stating, or perhaps just expressing, my own approval of it, on the

[31] *Human Society in Ethics and Politics*, p. 25.
[32] *Ibid.*, p. 55.
[33] *Ibid.*, p .116.

ground that its existence is or would be found generally satisfying. Right actions, as before, are defined in terms of their probable consequences. "An act of which, on the available evidence, the effects are likely to be better than those of any other act that is possible in the circumstances, is defined as 'right'; any other act is 'wrong'. What we 'ought' to do is, by definition, the act which is right."[34] Here it is understood that the better effects are those that yield "the greatest balance of satisfaction over dissatisfaction, or the smallest balance of dissatisfaction over satisfaction,"[35] independently of the question who enjoys the one or suffers the other. Russell goes on to say that "It is right to feel approval of a right act and disapproval of a wrong act."[36] If he is not being forgetful of his own definition, and using the word "right," in its first occurrence in this sentence, purely normatively, what he must mean is that the general acceptance of the rule that we are to aim at maximizing satisfaction will itself be likely to maximize satisfaction: and indeed this may very well be true.

Russell is a consistent utilitarian in that he draws no ethical distinction between the qualities of different forms of satisfaction. One is as good as another if the quantity of satisfaction is the same. In his case, however, this is less paradoxical than it sounds, because he is using the word "satisfaction" very widely to cover the fulfillment of any end. Presumably, there must be some enjoyment of the end attained for the word to be applicable, but the ends which yield the greatest satisfaction, in Russell's usage, are not necessarily those that cause the greatest enjoyment. They are rather those that we continue to wish to pursue. Russell is able to make this

[34] *Ibid.*
[35] *Ibid.*, p. 145.
[36] *Ibid.*, p. 116.

distinction, because, as we have seen, he does not fall into the common utilitarian error of assuming that all desire is for pleasure. Thus he finds it possible to admit that "some pleasures seem to us inherently preferable to others,"[36] without having to regard this as an argument against his view that all forms of satisfaction are equally valuable in themselves.

Even so, he still faces the objection that certain desires, such as the desire to inflict pain upon others, are intrinsically evil, and that there are things, such as freedom and justice, which have an intrinsic value independently of their being generally desired. Russell is sensitive to this objection, on account of his own love of freedom and hatred of cruelty and injustice, but he still tries to meet it in the stock utilitarian way. He has to say that the fulfillment of a sadist's desire to cause pain to others is *pro tanto* good, but that it is outweighed by the dissatisfaction of his victims. This argument appears to fail, or at any rate to have consequences which Russell would find unacceptable, in the case of the persecution of minorities, where many people find satisfaction in tormenting a few. One might try to deal with such cases by bringing in the dissatisfaction caused to those who disapprove of such conduct, on the dubious assumption that enough people do always know and disapprove of it to make the balance come out right, or by saying that the long-term effects of persecution are injurious to the society in which it is practiced: but neither of these expedients is altogether convincing. The trouble is that from the fact that the general satisfaction would be greater than it is if people were so constituted that they were habitually kind to one another, it does not follow that kindness is always a source of greater

[36] *Ibid.*, p. 117.

satisfaction than cruelty, if people are taken as they actually are.

Similarly, in the case of justice, Russell is able to argue that it is valuable as a means rather than an end,[37] because he considers it only in relation to the equal distribution of goods. On this point, he argues that equality is to be favored because of the discontent which inequality causes, but allows that there is something to be said for inequality in a society where it is generally accepted. He does not consider the difficulty, for his theory, of injustice in the legal sense, in a case where greater satisfaction would be caused by the condemnation than by the acquittal of an innocent man. There is no doubt at all on which side Russell's moral sentiments would lie: the problem is whether his theory can be made to fit them.

I think that one reason why Russell gets into these difficulties is that he insists on making ethics descriptive, because he wants to be able to say that ethical propositions are true or false "in the same sense as if they were propositions of science."[38] This is a departure from the view which he held in the 1930s that "a judgement of intrinsic value is to be interpreted, not as an assertion, but as an expression of desire, concerning the desires of mankind": so that, "When I say 'hatred is bad', I am really saying: 'Would that no one felt hatred.' "[39] If he had remained content with some such emotive or prescriptive view, he could still have made it a general rule that one should aim at maximizing satisfaction, but could have added the proviso that such things as justice and kindness were to be valued in themselves and in

[37] *Ibid.*, p. 133.
[38] *Ibid.*, p. 116.
[39] *Power*, p. 257. See also *Religion and Science*, p. 235.

some cases given an overriding value. This would have reflected his own moral outlook, which is not exclusively utilitarian. The utilitarian element is emphasized in his pronouncements on sexual morality, where he takes the humane and sensible view that we should feel free to do as we want, except when it causes harm to others, and that where there are children it is desirable that marriages should be stable, even at the cost of tolerating some sexual infidelity. Where his utilitarianism falters is, as we have seen, in his reaction to cruelty, injustice, and hypocrisy, and also in his scorn for myths and taboos, even if people find satisfaction in them. "There is something feeble," he says, "and a little contemptible, about a man who cannot face the perils of life without the help of comfortable myths."[40] Describing "the world that I should wish to see," he says that it is "one where emotions are strong but not destructive, and where, because they are acknowledged, they lead to no deception either of oneself or of others. Such a world would include love and friendship and the pursuit of art and knowledge. I cannot," he adds, "hope to satisfy those who want something more tigerish."[41]

It is because so many people do want something more tigerish that Russell's theory of ethics falls short as a descriptive theory. As a prescriptive theory, which is predominantly but not entirely utilitarian, I find it altogether acceptable.

B. RELIGION

There is a story that Russell was once asked at a public meeting what he would say if after his death he found himself confronted by his Maker. He replied without

[40] *Human Society in Ethics and Politics*, p. 219.
[41] *Ibid.*, p. 11.

hesitation, "I should say: 'God! Why did you make the evidence for your existence so insufficient?' "

This very well expresses Russell's attitude toward the question of the existence of the God of Christian theology. He does not find the proposition that such a being exists unintelligible, or logically impossible: he maintains only that there is not the slightest reason to think it true. In a lecture entitled "Why I am not a Christian," which he delivered in 1927 and subsequently published in a collection of essays under the same title, he briefly runs through some of the main arguments which have been thought to establish the existence of such a God and shows them all to be fallacious. Thus, the argument to a first cause is found to be inconsistent, since it starts with an assumption of universal causation and ends with the postulation of an uncaused cause. The argument that the existence of the laws of nature implies a law-giver is shown to rest upon an elementary confusion between the legal concept of law as a body of rules laid down by some authority, and the scientific concept of law as a description of what generally happens. It is further weakened, in Russell's opinion, by the fact that if we are to believe modern physics, the fundamental laws of nature are statistical. The argument that God is required to supply a ground for morality fails for the reason, which we have already noted,[42] that no moral system can be founded on authority; there is always need for the nontautological premise that what the authority enjoins is right. The argument that there must be a God to redress the balance of justice by allocating rewards and punishments in a future life simply begs the question. As Russell remarks, it is like arguing that if there are bad oranges at the top of a crate, there must be good oranges underneath to redress the balance. If there

[42] See above, p. 123.

is a preponderance of injustice in the world, this is an argument against the existence of a benevolent deity, rather than an argument for it.

A less frivolous argument is the argument from design, which relies on a supposed analogy between the organization of the universe and the organization of a manufactured article, like a clock, as support for the conclusion that the universe also had a manufacturer. But the trouble with this argument is that the analogy is false. There are many teleological systems within the universe, but we have no reason to think that the universe itself is a teleological system, let alone that it serves any benevolent purpose. As Russell puts it, in another essay,

> The second law of thermodynamics makes it scarcely possible to doubt that the universe is running down, and that ultimately nothing of the slightest interest will be possible anywhere. Of course, it is open to us to say that when that time comes God will wind up the machinery again; but if we do say this, we can base our assertion only upon faith, not upon one shred of scientific evidence. So far as scientific evidence goes, the universe has crawled by slow stages to a somewhat pitiful result on this earth, and is going to crawl by still more pitiful stages to a condition of universal death. If this is to be taken as evidence of purpose, I can only say that the purpose is one that does not appeal to me. I see no reason therefore to believe in any sort of God, however vague and however attenuated.[43]

In a broadcast debate with Father Copleston, the text of which is reproduced in *Why I am not a Christian*, Russell has a few words to say about the argument from contingency and the argument from religious experi-

[43] "Has Religion Made Useful Contributions to Civilization?," in *Why I am not a Christian*, pp. 24–25.

ence. The argument from contingency, as set out by Copleston, is that since nothing in the world contains the reason for its own existence, there must be a necessary being, external to the world, which both contains the reason for its own existence and supplies the reason why the world exists. This is not so obviously fallacious as the so-called ontological argument, which comes down to saying that merely by defining God as a necessary being we can ensure that he necessarily exists, but it rests on a similar mistake. To begin with, as Russell points out, necessity is properly ascribed not to objects but to propositions. To talk of the existence of a necessary being, or one which contains the reason for its own existence, is a loose way of claiming that there is something which is such that the proposition that it exists is necessarily true. But then the validity of this claim needs to be established. It certainly does not follow from the fact that empirical existential propositions are contingent.

The feeling behind this argument is that there must be an explanation why the world exists. But in the first place the postulation of a deity does not provide an explanation, unless we can also explain why he made the world, and then we run into all the difficulties which we saw to be fatal to the argument from design. In the second place, as Russell argues, the demand for an explanation of everything is incoherent. Facts are explained by theories and theories by more general theories, but this process must stop somewhere. It is more rational, therefore, to be provisionally content with an empirical theory, which fulfills its function, than to fabricate a metaphysical theory, which does not.

The argument from religious experience is not favored by Copleston, though he attaches some weight to it. He admits the objection, which Russell raises, that not every experience of this kind is cognitive. The experi-

ences which have led men to believe that they were seeing Satan were as vivid as those which have led men to
believe that they were seeing God. The difficulty is to
find a criterion for deciding when such an experience is
to be held to be veridical. An attempt might be made to
formulate a criterion in terms of the coherence of the
accounts which mystics give of their experiences, but
the incoherence of their language makes this difficult to
determine; and, as Russell points out in his book on
Religion and Science, when they do appear to agree
upon a proposition, such as that everything is one, or
that time is unreal, it is usually a proposition that is
literally false. In any case, even if there were enough
consensus among mystics for it to be reasonable to talk
of their apprehending some existent object, the effect
would only be to widen our conception of the world.
It would provide no evidence at all for the truth of such
propositions as that the world had a benevolent creator.

The Christian religion encounters all the intellectual
difficulties which attend the belief in a transcendent
deity, together with many that it has made for itself.
Russell is derisively scornful of its superstitious ritual—
"The Roman Catholic Church holds that a priest can
turn a piece of bread into the Body and Blood of Christ
by talking Latin to it"[44]—of its irrational taboos—"We
are told not to work on Saturdays, and Protestants take
this to mean that we are not to play on Sundays. But
the same sublime authority is attributed to the new
prohibition as to the old"[45]—and of the way in which
its custodians, at least until quite recent times, have
attempted to frustrate almost every important scientific
advance: "Works teaching that the earth moves

[44] *Education and the Social Order*, pp. 70–71.
[45] "What I Believe," in *Why I am not a Christian*, p. 52.

remained on the Index till 1835."[46] "In Spanish universities, the circulation of the blood was still denied at the end of the eighteenth century."[47] Above all, he is revolted by the intellectual and moral dishonesty which Christian apologists display in trying to avoid the conclusion that if the world was created by an omnipotent and omniscient being, he is ultimately responsible for all the misery and suffering that it contains. The belief that suffering is a purification from sin would not, in any decent man, survive a visit to a children's hospital. As Russell puts it, "No man who believes that all is for the best in this suffering world can keep his ethical values unimpaired, since he is always having to find excuses for pain and misery."[48]

Not only does Russell not believe in the divinity of Christ: he does not agree that Christ, as depicted in the Gospels, was a supremely good man. Those who consider him so think mainly of the Sermon on the Mount: they forget the vindictiveness shown towards his opponents, the threats of fiery furnaces and the weeping and gnashing of teeth, the consignment of sinners to eternal punishment. There is no such vein of cruelty in what we are told of Buddha or of Socrates. Now that a literal belief in Hell has ceased to be either intellectually or morally respectable, we are told that Christ's more bloodthirsty sayings are either not authentic or not intended to be taken literally. There is, however, no historical justification for discriminating between them and the rest of his reputed teaching.

We should observe also that historically it is the more intolerant aspects of Christ's teaching that have had by

[46] *Religion and Science*, p. 41.
[47] *Ibid.*, p. 103.
[48] *Why I am not a Christian*, p. 23.

far the greater influence, at least on the practice of the organized Christian churches. As Russell puts it, "Christianity has been distinguished from other religions by its greater readiness for persecution."[49] Christians have repeatedly persecuted heretics, persecuted Jews, persecuted freethinkers, persecuted one another, often with the greatest refinements of cruelty. They have tortured and killed thousands of innocent women on the pretext that they were witches—does it not say in the Bible that thou shalt not suffer a witch to live?—and made the lives of innumerable children wretched by their sadistic application of the preposterous doctrine of original sin. Even in our own time, the Roman Catholic Church endeavors to ensure, by its opposition to birth control, that "a life of torture is inflicted upon millions of human beings who ought never to have existed, merely because it is supposed that sexual intercourse is wicked unless it is accompanied by desire for offspring, but not wicked when this desire is present, even though the offspring is humanly certain to be wretched."[50] If Christians, in general, have become more humane, this is mainly due, in Russell's opinion, to the pressure exerted by freethinkers. "The whole contention that Christianity has had an elevating moral influence can only be maintained by wholesale ignoring or falsification of the historical evidence."[51]

This is to some extent unfair, since it ignores the part played by individual Christians in such moral advances as the abolition of the slave trade, the more humane treatment of prisoners, the reform in the conditions of child labor, and, at the present time, the opposition to racial discrimination. The fact remains, however, that

[49] *Ibid.*, p. 176.
[50] *Ibid.*, pp. 52–53.
[51] *Ibid.*, p. 176.

until very recently, such reforms have generally been opposed by the Christian hierarchy, which has seldom been reluctant to render unto Caesar the things that are Caesar's, except when it has been a question of its own riches and power. This is not to argue that the moral failings, which Christians share with others, prove Christianity untrue. On the theological side, the grounds for not believing it are rational. On the moral side, the charge is that the moral failings find an apparent sanction in a part of Christian teaching; above all, in the doctrine of sin and retribution, and in the parable of the sheep and the goats, the restriction of salvation to the faithful, which has too often outweighed the noble idea of the brotherhood of man.

The belief in an afterlife is normally the outcome of religious belief, but it is not logically dependent on it. Russell grants that "There would be disembodied mind if there were groups of events connected according to the laws of psychology, but not according to the laws of physics,"[52] and if the admittedly doubtful point be conceded that it is possible to define self-identity in terms of relations between experiences, without reference to bodily identity, it is conceivable that such a disembodied mind should be psychologically continuous with one that was previously embodied. The question then becomes empirical. On the one hand there are the phenomena studied in psychical research, which are hard to evaluate, but may perhaps be seen as favoring the hypothesis of survival; on the other, there is very strong evidence that all our mental states are causally dependent upon bodily states, or, to put it in Russell's terms, that events are connected according to the laws of psychology only when they are also connected accord-

[52] "Mind and Matter," *Portraits from Memory*, p. 149 (Readers Union Edition, p. 155).

monarch commands unquestioning obedience means that he has no prudential motive for ruling benevolently. Self-interest may lead him to bestow favor on the small group to whom he delegates power; but within very large limits, he can afford to be indifferent to the welfare of the mass of his subjects. The monarchy is threatened only when, through cultural and economic changes, some group other than that on which the sovereign has been relying finds itself sufficiently powerful, and its interests sufficiently neglected, for it to overcome its habit of obedience. Thus, both in England and France, the reign of absolute monarchy came to an end because of the opposition of the rising middle class.

Another weakness of the monarchical system lies in the difficulty of securing a satisfactory principle of succession. The dangers are greatest when the succession, as in the later Roman Empire, is not hereditary. Hereditary succession diminishes, without wholly excluding, the risk of civil war, but it has the drawback that it produces rulers who are unfit for their position. If they are sufficiently incapable, the tendency is for power to pass irrevocably into the hands of their ministers, so that even if the form of monarchy is retained, it ceases to be absolute.

"The natural successor," as Russell says, "to absolute monarchy is oligarchy."[57] This can take various forms. "It may be the rule of a hereditary aristocracy, of the rich, or of a Church or political party."[58] As Russell sees it, "A hereditary landed aristocracy is apt to be conservative, proud, stupid, and rather brutal,"[59] with the result that it loses power to the higher bourgeoisie. The government of the rich "which prevailed in all the

[57] Ibid., p. 193.
[58] Ibid.
[59] Ibid.

free cities of the Middle Ages, and survived in Venice until Napoleon extinguished it" is said by Russell to "have been, on the whole, more enlightened and astute than any others known to history,"[60] but he does not attribute the same capacity to "the modern industrial magnate." The rule of a political party, such as the Fascists or the Communists, is assimilated to that of the church, because of the party's dogmatic acceptance of some political creed. The merits of this form of rule are that "the believers form a nucleus for social cohesion"[61] and that except when the creed is such as to attract only adventurers and stupid people "they are almost sure to be more energetic and politically conscious than the average of the population."[62] Its great demerit is that it is inimical to liberty. Being convinced of its possession of the truth, the oligarchy does not tolerate dissent; neither does it permit the development of institutions which might threaten its monopoly of power. Even when it is theoretically committed to seeing its rule as a transitional stage toward a more democratic form of government, it finds reasons for perpetuating itself, as the example of Soviet Russia has conspicuously shown.

Though he has little sympathy for what he calls theocratic oligarchies, Russell allows that a strong case could have been made for an oligarchic form of government, implying the existence of a privileged, comparatively leisured, class, in societies where the material conditions were such that the enjoyment of wealth and leisure was possible only for a small minority. "So long," he says, "as it was necessary to the bare subsistence of the human race that most men should work very long hours for a

[60] *Ibid.*
[61] *Ibid.*, p. 195.
[62] *Ibid.*, pp. 195–96.

pittance, so long no civilization was possible except an aristocratic one; if there were to be men with sufficient leisure for any mental life, there had to be others who were sacrificed for the good of the few."[63] No doubt, it was unjust that the majority should be so sacrificed, but it could be argued that a measure of civilization, which depended on this injustice, was better than no civilization at all. This situation, however, no longer obtains. If we made an intelligent use of all the resources of modern technology, "we could," in Russell's opinion, "within twenty years, abolish all abject poverty, quite half the illness in the world, the whole economic slavery which binds down nine-tenths of our population: we could fill the world with beauty and joy, and secure the reign of universal peace."[64] This passage, which was written in 1917, may sound absurdly optimistic, but at least we can accept the underlying assumption that in an industrially developed country, where the practice of birth control limits the growth of population, there is now no economic reason for the persistence of poverty or of long hours of labor, or of any lack of the opportunity to receive a good education; and in these circumstances the argument that civilization requires the existence of a privileged leisure class loses its force. Since it is likely that a more democratic form of government will lead to a more even distribution both of material goods and of the power to enjoy what Russell calls some "mental life," the principle of justice speaks strongly in its favor.

In any large-scale society, only a limited number of persons can effectively exercise power, and for this reason the difference between an oligarchic and a democratic form of government can in any case be only a difference of degree. As Russell puts it, "a government

[63] *Political Ideals* (1917), p. 35.
[64] *Ibid.*, p. 25.

is usually called 'democratic' if a fairly large percentage of the population has a share of political power,"[65] but both the percentage and the extent and nature of the share may vary quite considerably. Thus, in ancient Athens the ordinary citizen could if he wished take a direct part in the government of the city: if the lot fell on him, he could even hold office: but women were excluded from the franchise, and a high proportion of the male population consisted of foreign residents and slaves who had no part at all in government. In contemporary England, almost every adult has the right to vote, to adhere to a political party, and to stand for election if he can afford it, but the amount of effective power that this gives him may be very small. Even in the uncommonly favorable case in which he contrives to get himself elected to Parliament and his own party is in power, he may have very little voice in deciding what is done. The party's program, as Russell says, "is decided in a manner which is nominally democratic, but is very much influenced by a small number of wire-pullers. It is left," he continues, "to the leaders to decide, in their parliamentary or governmental activities, whether they shall attempt to carry out the programme; if they decide not to do so, it is the duty of their followers to support their breach of faith by their votes, while denying, in their speeches, that it has taken place. It is this system that has given to leaders the power to thwart their rank-and-file supporters, and to advocate reforms without having to enact them."[66]

This is a cynical but not, I fear, a wholly false account of the way in which representative government is conducted: and it has not become any the less true in the thirty-three years since Russell wrote it. It should, how-

[65] *Power*, p. 197.
[66] *Ibid.*, p. 177.

ever, be added that it commonly does not escape people's notice that the reforms have not been enacted, and that a likely consequence of this is that the leaders who have failed to keep their promises will eventually suffer at least a temporary loss of power. The ordinary citizen may not have much positive say in the management of his country's affairs, but at least he has a fair hope of exercising enough negative control to ensure that his interests are not totally neglected. Democracy, as Russell says, "does not ensure good government, but it prevents certain evils": [67] not the least of them being the possession by an incompetent or unjust government of a permanent tenure of power.

Democracy, at least in England and America, is associated with what Russell calls the doctrine of personal liberty. "This doctrine," he says, "in practice, consists of two parts, on the one hand that a man shall not be punished except by due process of law, and on the other hand that there shall be a sphere in which a man's actions are not to be subject to governmental control. This sphere includes free speech, a free press and religious freedom. It used to include freedom of economic enterprise."[68] Russell admits that these freedoms are all subject to limitation. Even the freedom of expression, to which he attaches very high importance, may have to be curtailed when it threatens the security of the state. "It is not difficult," he says, "for a government to concede freedom of thought when it can rely upon loyalty in action; but when it cannot, the matter is more difficult."[69] The problem of reconciling personal freedom with stable and efficient government is, indeed, one that greatly troubled Russell, but I cannot find that he con-

---

[67] *Ibid.*, p. 286.
[68] *Unpopular Essays* (1950), p. 183.
[69] *Power*, p. 155.

tributed much toward solving it. Perhaps it is a problem that can have no general solution.

As for the freedom of economic enterprise, Russell is in favor of it to the extent that he is opposed to concentrations of economic power, whether it be in the hands of the state or in those of private cartels. At the same time, he wishes to set severe limitations on the possession and use of private property. He does not dissent from the principle that a man should enjoy the fruits of his own labor, but he sees no justification for inherited wealth; and even in the rare cases where it does not depend upon inherited wealth, he is opposed to the private ownership of big businesses or of land.

Partly for these reasons, Russell is willing to describe himself as a socialist, especially in his earlier political writings, but he differs from the ordinary run of socialists in that he wishes to diminish rather than increase the power of the state. He thinks that "the modern great State" is too much concerned with "the promotion of efficiency in war," in which it is more likely to engage as the result of the measures which it takes for its security, and that it is also "harmful from its vastness and the resulting sense of individual helplessness."[70] "Modern States," he says, "as opposed to the small city States of ancient Greece or mediaeval Italy, leave little room for initiative, and fail to develop in most men any sense of ability to control their political destinies. The few men who achieve power in such States are men of abnormal ambition and thirst for dominion, combined with skill in cajolery and subtlety in negotiation. All the rest are dwarfed by knowledge of their own impotence."[71]

Russell believes that we should look to the state to diminish economic injustice, but does not think that

---

[70] *Principles of Social Reconstruction*, pp. 59–60.
[71] *Ibid.*, p. 61.

this is likely to be achieved by the method of nationalizing industries. He takes as an example the state purchase of railways. Having remarked that if the owners of railway shares are adequately compensated, it will not result in any extensive redistribution of income, he continues as follows:

> There is equally little advance toward freedom. The men employed on the railway have no more voice than they had before in the management of the railway, or in the wages and conditions of work. Instead of having to fight the directors, with the possibility of an appeal to the government, they now have to fight the government directly; and experience does not lead to the view that a government department has any special tenderness towards the claims of labour. If they strike, they have to contend against the whole organized power of the state, which they can only do successfully if they happen to have a strong public opinion on their side. In view of the influence which the state can always exercise on the press, public opinion is likely to be biased against them, particularly when a nominally progressive government is in power. . . .
> And there is no real advance towards democracy. The administration of the railways will be in the hands of officials whose bias and associations separate them from labour, and who will develop an autocratic temper through the habit of power. The democratic machinery by which these officials are normally controlled is cumbrous and remote, and can only be brought into operation on first-class issues which rouse the interest of the whole nation. Even then it is very likely that the superior education of the officials and the government, combined with the advantages of their position, will enable them to mislead the public as to the issues, and alienate the general sympathy even from the most excellent cause."[72]

[72] *Political Ideals* (1917), pp. 44–46.

When it is considered that this passage was written in 1917, thirty years before the nationalization of the railways actually took place in England, it seems astonishingly prescient.

The form of socialism for which Russell had the most sympathy is one to which little attention has been paid in England since the First World War, probably, no doubt, because the Italian Fascists drew some inspiration from it, although they greatly perverted it. It was called Guild Socialism and was a blend of State Socialism and the theory of government through trade unions which the French, who were its chief exponents, called Syndicalism. Its main principles were that each factory should elect its own managers; that all the factories in a given industry should be federated into a Guild, which would pay a tax to the state in return for the supply of the means of production, would apportion wages and the hours of labor within the industry, and would arrange for the marketing of its products; that the Guilds should be federated into a Congress which would be of equal standing with a Parliament of consumers which would be elected on a constituency basis; and that a Joint Committee of Parliament and the Guild Congress should be the ultimate sovereign body, fixing prices and taxes and serving as the final court of appeal in all matters involving the interests of consumers and producers alike: it would be, for example, the responsibility of this Committee to ensure that none of the Guilds set its own interests above those of the community.

In his book *Roads to Freedom*, in which he outlines this system, Russell says that he believes it to be "the best hitherto proposed, and the one most likely to secure liberty without the constant appeals to violence which are to be feared under a purely Anarchist regime."[73]

---

[73] *Roads to Freedom*, p. 92.

He does not discuss in any detail how its principles would apply to nonindustrial workers, but does express some fear that the formation of guilds of artists and writers might lead to the suppression of original work. To accommodate people of this sort, as well as those who do not care to do any kind of work, Russell proposes "that a certain small income, sufficient for necessaries should be secured to all, whether they work or not, and that a larger income—as much larger as might be warranted by the total amount of commodities produced, should be given to those who are willing to engage in some work which the community recognizes as useful."[74] This proposal would hardly be practicable if the number of those who did not wish to work or wished to do work that was not recognized as useful were at all large, but Russell believed that the lure of the greater luxury which would be obtainable through doing useful work, as well as the improved conditions of work under the system of Guild Socialism, would be sufficient to keep it manageably small.

The idea of there being "local government by trades as well as by areas"[75] is to be found also in Russell's *Principles of Social Reconstruction*, which was published in 1916, two years before *Roads to Freedom*. Here too, he sees devolution as the means of avoiding the concentration of too much power in the central government, arguing that "The positive purposes of the State, over and above the preservation of order, ought as far as possible to be carried out, not by the State itself, but by independent organizations which should be left completely free so long as they satisfied the State that they were not falling below a necessary minimum."[76] It

[74] *Ibid.*, pp. 119–20.
[75] *Principles of Social Reconstruction*, p. 72.
[76] *Ibid.*, p. 75.

would be the duty of the state to see that adequate standards were maintained in respect to health, education, and scientific research, but otherwise our aim should be "to give every man a sphere of political activity small enough for his interest and his capacity, and to confine the functions of the State as far as possible, to the maintenance of peace among rival interests,"[77] looking to it also to diminish economic injustice.

In the furtherance of justice, Russell makes the original proposal that the expense of children, that is to say their food and clothing and education, should be borne wholly by the community. He does not make it a condition that their parents should be married to one another but only that they should be "physically and mentally sound in all ways likely to affect the children."[78] Those who were not certified as being sound in this way would not be debarred from having children but they would have to pay for them themselves. In addition, "a woman who is capable of earning money, and who abandons wage-earning for motherhood, ought to receive from the State as nearly as possible what she would have received if she had not had children."[79] How these measures could be afforded is a question into which Russell does not enter.

In his later political writings Russell is more concerned with the relations between states than with questions of internal organization, but he continues to issue warnings against the dangers of entrusting too much power to the state. In his book on *Power*, he says that while "public ownership and control of all large-scale industry and finance is a *necessary* condition for the taming of power, it is far from being a *sufficient* condi-

[77] *Ibid.*, pp. 74–75.
[78] *Ibid.*, p. 185.
[79] *Ibid.*, p. 184.

tion. It needs to be supplemented by a democracy, more thorough-going, more carefully safeguarded against official tyranny, and with more deliberate provision for freedom of propaganda, than any purely political democracy that has ever existed."[80] Among these safeguards are the restraints to be put upon the police, which already in the 1930s Russell saw as a body tending in most countries to become too much of a law unto itself. In view of the widespread practice of obtaining confessions by torture, he regarded it as essential that a confession should never, in any circumstances, be accepted as evidence, and he made the suggestion that there should be two police forces, "one designed, as at present, to prove guilt, the other to prove innocence"[81] and a public defender of equal legal eminence to the public prosecutor. In cases where the prosecuting police were charged with crimes committed in the execution of their duty, the defending police would organize their prosecution. This is a nice idea but I do not expect to see it realized.

In spite of his love of England, Russell was a very great enemy to nationalism. In *Power*, which came out shortly before the Second World War, he spoke of it as "a stupid ideal,"[82] which was bringing Europe to ruin, and in an earlier work he described it as "undoubtedly the most dangerous vice of our time—far more dangerous than drunkenness, or drugs, or commercial dishonesty, or any of the other vices against which a conventional moral education is directed."[83] After the Second World War, as we have seen, he increasingly saw the nationalistic temper of Soviet Russia and still more of the United States as likely to provoke a third world war,

[80] *Power*, p. 303.
[81] *Ibid.*, p. 296.
[82] *Ibid.*, p. 158.
[83] *Education and the Social Order* (1932), p. 138.

which the use of atomic weapons would render far more terrible. As I said earlier,[84] the only long-term assurance that he could find against the continuing threat of such a disaster was the institution of a world government, which would have the monopoly of armed force. He recognized the dangers of such a concentration of power, but hoped that they could be met by the concession to local areas of as large a measure of autonomy as was consistent with their not being fully sovereign. And even if the dangers were not entirely met, he thought this to be a lesser evil than the occurrence of global wars. So much, indeed, did he see the prevention of war as the main function of a world-state that he thought that this should be allowed to override considerations of abstract justice. Thus, in *Principles of Social Reconstruction* he wrote that "A world-State or federation of States, if it is to be successful, will have to decide questions, not by the legal maxims which would be applied by the Hague tribunal, but as far as possible in the same sense in which they would be decided by war. The function of authority should be to render the appeal to force unnecessary, not to give decisions contrary to those which would be reached by force."[85] This sounds a harsh saying, but it rests on the plausible assumption that the stronger parties to the federation would not meekly accept decisions that went against what they conceived to be their interests. If they retained their separate armies, this would almost certainly be so, as the history of the League of Nations showed, and even if they had renounced them, it might still be so in the early stages of a world government, when the members of its armed forces might still retain their national sentiments. On the other hand, if the world government were well estab-

[84] See above, p. 25.
[85] *Principles of Social Reconstruction*, p. 66.

lished, universally recognized as sovereign, and endowed with a monopoly of force, there would seem to be no good reason why it should not deal impartially with the interests of what had previously been separate states.

The difficult question is how such an institution is ever to come into being. One way in which it might happen would be for one of the great powers to obtain dominion over all the rest, and Russell appears consistently to have regarded this as a possibility which would in the long run be preferable to the continued existence of separate sovereign states. Thus, in his book on *Education and the Social Order*, which was published in 1932, having argued that "until the issue between communism and capitalism is decided, world peace cannot be secure, whatever machinery may be created," and finding it "difficult to see how this issue can be decided except by the victory of communism, at any rate throughout Europe,"[86] he was disposed to welcome this result, in spite of his dislike of the Soviet regime. Later on he came to look upon the victory of communism as being both less probable and less easy to acquiesce in, but he still seems to have considered it a price worth paying for the end of international anarchy. This comes out in *New Hopes for a Changing World*, a book published in 1951, in which he argues:

> Just as the substitution of orderly government for monarchy in the Middle Ages depended upon the victory of the royal power, so the substitution of order for anarchy in international relations, if it comes about, will come about through the superior power of some one nation or group of nations. And only after such a single Government has been constituted will it be possible for the evolution towards a democratic form of international Government to begin.[87]

[86] *Education and the Social Order*, pp. 234–35.
[87] *New Hopes for a Changing World*, p. 77.

Russell thought that this process of evolution might take a century or so, by which time the government would have begun to "command that degree of respect that will make it possible to base its power upon law and sentiment rather than upon force": it could then become democratic. He admitted that "it would be far better to have an international Government constituted by agreement,"[88] but believed that the appeal of nationalism and men's anarchic impulses were still too strong for this to be a serious possibility.

In taking this position, Russell was responding to his belief that no evil was greater than those which were likely to result from the continuance of large-scale wars and that the institution of a world government was the only sure way to prevent them from recurring. The difficulty was that except in the improbable event of its being swift and decisive, the war which would be needed to put a single power, or group of powers, into the position of constituting a world government would precipitate the evils which such a government was intended to prevent. Consequently, Russell was led to advocate a policy of unilateral disarmament, which would have the effect of presenting whichever side did not disarm with a military hegemony. The probability, however, that either side would adopt such a policy was even smaller than the probability that an international government would be instituted by mutual agreement.

That Russell reached this impasse was, I think, mainly due to his overestimating the current likelihood of a global nuclear war and correspondingly underestimating the merits of the old theory of the balance of power. A world government would, in my view, be desirable, and the improvement in communications, and the increasing economic interdependence of different areas, make its

[88] *Ibid.*, pp. 77–78.

attainment by voluntary agreement less improbable than it has so far been. Nevertheless this is at best a long-term hope. In the meantime, a period of relatively peaceful coexistence between the major powers, notwithstanding all its dangers, seems to me more probable and more desirable than the forcible acquisition by any single power of a world empire.

In a memoir in which he was describing the intellectual climate of Cambridge before the First World War, Maynard Keynes said of Russell that "Bertie in particular sustained simultaneously a pair of opinions ludicrously incompatible. He held that in fact human affairs were carried on after a most irrational fashion, but that the remedy was quite simple and easy, since all we had to do was to carry them on rationally."[88] Whether or not this was a fair criticism of the way in which Russell talked at that time, it does not do justice to his later views. We have seen that he did take some account of the psychological obstacles which prevented men from conducting their affairs in a rational manner. Nevertheless, I think that, except perhaps at the very end of his life, he did underrate the difficulty of weaning men away from their irrational beliefs, and perhaps overestimated their capacity to pursue even a policy of enlightened self-interest. In these respects he resembled his godfather, John Stuart Mill.

This was not the only way in which Russell came close to Mill. We have seen that he also shared his utilitarianism, his concern for the rights of women, his belief that social justice was hardly possible without some form of socialism, and his philosophical empiricism. Mill paid more attention than Russell to the social sciences, and his contributions to the theory of morals and politics are the more solid. On the other hand, Russell was much

[88] J. M. Keynes, *Two Memoirs*, p. 102.

the better logician, and the more original and far-seeing philosopher. In his later years, Mill was known as the saint of Rationalism. Bertrand Russell would not have wished to be called a saint of any description; but he was a great and good man.

SHORT BIBLIOGRAPHY

INDEX

SHORT BIBLIOGRAPHY

A. SELECTED WORKS BY BERTRAND RUSSELL*

1. Philosophical

A Critical Exposition of the Philosophy of Leibniz. 1900.
The Principles of Mathematics. 1903.
Principia Mathematica, with A. N. Whitehead. 3 volumes.
    1910, 1912, and 1913.
The Problems of Philosophy. 1912.
Our Knowledge of the External World. 1914.
Mysticism and Logic. 1917.
The Analysis of Mind. 1921.
The Analysis of Matter. 1927.
An Outline of Philosophy. 1927.
An Inquiry into Meaning and Truth. 1940.
A History of Western Philosophy. 1945.
Human Knowledge: Its Scope and Limits. 1948.
Logic and Knowledge. 1956.
My Philosophical Development. 1959.

2. Political and Social

Principles of Social Reconstruction. 1916.
Roads to Freedom. 1918.

* Dates refer to the first English edition.

The Practice and Theory of Bolshevism. 1920.
On Education. 1926.
Why I am not a Christian. 1927.
Sceptical Essays. 1928.
Marriage and Morals. 1929.
The Conquest of Happiness. 1930.
Education and the Social Order. 1932.
Power. 1938.
Authority and the Individual. 1949.
New Hopes for a Changing World. 1951.
Human Society in Ethics and Politics. 1954.

3. *Biographical*

The Amberley Papers, with Patricia Russell. 2 volumes.
    1937.
Portraits from Memory. 1956.
Autobiography. 3 volumes. 1967, 1968, and 1969.

B. Books about Bertrand Russell

1. *Philosophical*

Ayer, A. J. *Russell and Moore: The Analytical Heritage.*
    New York: Macmillan, 1971.
Pears, D. F. *Bertrand Russell and the British Tradition in
    Philosophy.* New York: Random House, 1967.
Schilpp, Paul, ed. *The Philosophy of Bertrand Russell.* New
    York: Harper, 1962, 1963.
Watling, John. *Bertrand Russell.* New York: British Book
    Centre, 1971.

2. *Biographical*

Crawshay-Williams, Rupert. *Russell Remembered.* New
    York: Oxford University Press, 1970.
Hardy, G. H. *Bertrand Russell and Trinity.* New York: Ox-
    ford University Press, 1970.
Wood, Alan. *Bertrand Russell, the Passionate Skeptic.* New
    York: Simon and Schuster, 1958.

INDEX

Abstract ideas, 30
Acquaintance, knowledge by, 10, 30–35, 86–87
After-life, improbability of, 137–38
Agnosticism, Russell's, 8–9, 131–34
ALLEN, Clifford, Lord Allen of Hurtwood, 13
AMBERLEY, 1st Viscount, 2
AMBERLEY, Viscountess, 2
Ambiguity, systematic, 47
Analogy, postulate of, 99, 101–102
Analytic propositions, 41–42, 112
Anarchism, 147
APOSTLES, Society of the, 4
Argument, of a function, 46
Atomic facts, 113
Atomic objects, 104, 112
Atomic warfare, 25, 151
Atomicity, principle of, 112
Authority, not a ground for morality, 123, 131

BALFOUR, Arthur James, 15
BARNES, Albert C., 22
Basic facts, 31–32
Basic propositions, 67

Belief, Russell's analysis of, 59–64
BERKELEY, George, 11, 58, 70, 106
BLACK, Dora, see RUSSELL, Dora
Brain and Mind, Russell's identification of, 115–16
BRYN MAWR COLLEGE, 22
BUDDHA, 135

CALIFORNIA, UNIVERSITY OF, 20
CAMBRIDGE, UNIVERSITY OF, 3, 5, 15, 18, 154
CARNAP, Rudolf, 29
CARROLL, Lewis, 41
Causal laws, as differentiating mind from matter, 88, 114–15
Causal lines, separable, postulate of, 99–100, 102
Causation, Russell's theory of, 84, 91–92, 107; mnemic, 91–92
Cause, first, argument to a, 131
CHICAGO, UNIVERSITY OF, 20
CHRIST, 135–36

Christianity, Russell's disapproval of, 134–37
Classes, 42–43; and numbers, 36–37, 42; antinomy concerning, 44, 47; as logical fictions, 33, 43, 48, 55; similarity of, 36, 38
Committee of 100, the, 26
Common sense, Russell's opinion of, 74, 83–85
Communism, Russell's attitude toward, 17–18, 23, 141, 152
Compresence, 88, 108–10; complete complexes of, 109–11
Concepts, 54
Conjunction, 39
CONRAD, Joseph, 17
Conscience, Russell's attitude to, 119, 124
Contingency, argument from, 132–33
Continuants, material, 100
Continuity: sensible, 88; spatio-temporal, postulate of, 92, 99–100, 102
COPLESTON, Frederick, 132–33
Correspondence theory of truth, 64–66
Credibility, degrees of, 95, 98–99

Democracy, 142–44
Demonstratives, 53, 57–58, 108
Denotation, 10, 49–51, 57
DESCARTES, René, 30, 87, 114
Description, knowledge by, 10, 32–35, 114–15
Descriptions, Russell's theory of, 10, 47, 48–58, 105
Design, argument from, 132
Determinism, and free-will, 120–21
Disarmament: nuclear, campaign for, 26; unilateral, Russell's advocacy of, 153

Disjunction, 39
Dreams, 80
DUKHOBORS, the, 124

EDWARDS, Paul, 21
Egocentric particulars, 58
Egoism, 123–24
EINSTEIN, Albert, 20, 23, 25–26
ELIOT, T. S., 11
Emotive theory of ethics, 129
Empirical propositions, uncertainty of, 92–93, 116
Empiricism, Russell's, 11, 18, 29, 154
EPIMENIDES, 44–45
Ethics, Russell's theories of, 117–30
EUCLID, 3, 30, 38
Events: as complexes of qualities, 33, 113; constitute instants, 34; mental and physical, 114–16; reality of, 33, 113
Existence: as property of concepts, 54; whether a predicate, 55
Extensionality, 39, 59

FABIANS, 8
Facts: atomic, 113; reality of, 33, 112–13
Familiarity, feelings of, 90–91
Fascism, 141, 157
Feelings, 30, 87, 90–92, 108, 114–15
FINCH, Edith, *see* RUSSELL, Edith
Free will: Russell's account of, 120–22; believed by him to presuppose determinism, 121
FREGE, Gottlob, 3, 44, 54

Geometry, 3, 38–39
GEORGE IV, King, 49
GEORGE VI, King, 24
GÖDEL, Kurt, 23
GOLDSTEIN, 21

Good, Russell's accounts of
the concept, 118, 126–27
GOODMAN, Nelson, 95
Guild Socialism, 147–48

HAGUE TRIBUNAL, the, 151
HARDY, G. H., 14
HARVARD UNIVERSITY, 11,
14, 22
HEARST, William Randolph,
19
Hedonism, 123–24
HEGEL, G. W. F., 6
Hegelians, 50
Hegelianism, Russell's
early, 5
Horizontal inference, *see*
Inference
HUME, David, 11, 27, 29, 33,
84, 87, 89, 92–93, 106–
107, 121, 125

Identity of indiscernibles,
principle of the, 108, 110
Identity, personal, 88–89, 91
Illusion, argument from,
72–75
Image propositions, *see*
Propositions
Images, 87, 90–92, 108,
114–16
Implication, 39
Incomplete symbols, 50–52
Individuation, methods of
obtaining, 111–12
Individuals, 44–45
Induction, 23, 90, 95;
principle of, 93–94;
Russell's theory of, 92–102
Inferred entities, 34–35
Infinity, axiom of, 38
Instants, 34
Intentional objects, 60–62
Intrinsic properties, 74
Intuitionism, ethical, 118,
122–23

JAMES, William, 88
JESUITS, 124
JOHNSON, L. B., 26
JOLIOT-CURIE, F., 26
Judgment, Russell's theory
of, *see* Belief
Justice, Russell's account of,
129

KANT, Immanuel, 6, 124–25
KAY, Mrs., 21
KENNEDY, John F., 26
KEYNES, J. M., 98–99, 154
Knowledge: by acquaintance,
10, 30–35; by description,
10, 32–35, 114–15;
Russell's theory of, 54,
69–102

LA GUARDIA, Mayor, 21
Large numbers, law of, 97–98
LAWRENCE, D. H., 12–13
League of Nations, the, 151
LEIBNITZ, G. W., 6, 31, 78
Leisured class, argument for
a, 141–42
Liberty, political, 141, 144–
45
Linguistic philosophy,
Russell's disapproval of,
23
LOCKE, John, 11, 29–30, 32,
69, 120
Logic: and mathematics, 6,
35–39; Russell and White-
head's system of, 39–40;
status of propositions of,
41–42
Logical atomism, 15, 103–
104, 112
Logical constants, 39–40
Logical constructions, 35, 77,
82
Logical fictions, 33, 55, 71,
104
LOGICAL POSITIVISTS, 47
Logically proper names,
see Names
LONDON SCHOOL OF
ECONOMICS, 20

MALLESON, Lady Constance, 13, 16
MALLESON, Miles, 13
Mathematics: philosophy of, 6, 35; Russell's reduction of to logic, 6, 35–39
McGEEHAN, Judge, 21
McMASTERS UNIVERSITY, 26
McTAGGART, J. E., 4–6
Meaning, behavioral theory of, 67
MEINONG, A., 64
Memory: Russell's analysis of, 32, 89–92; and personal identity, 88–89; justification of, 90
Mental acts, Russell's rejection of, 60, 71, 89
MILL, John Stuart, 2, 11, 29, 154–55
Mind: and matter, 112–16; and brain, 115–16
Minds, constitution of, 87–88
MINTO, 2nd Earl of, 3
Mnemic causation, 91–92
Monarchism, 139–40
MOORE, G. E., 3, 6, 20, 29, 55, 69, 117–18
Moral actions, 119
MORMONS, 124
MORRELL, Lady Ottoline, 10–11, 16
MURRAY, Gilbert, 12
Mysticism, 8, 134

Naïve realism, Russell's rejection of, 74–75
Names: Russell's theory of, 50, 53, 57–58, 105; logically proper, 53–54, 58, 104–105; ordinary proper, 53, 57
NAPOLEON I, 141
Nationalism, Russell's dislike of, 150–51
Nationalization, Russell's comments on, 146–47
Necessity, a property of propositions, 133
Negation, 39

Neutral monism, 114, 116
Neutral stuff, 114
NICOD, Jean, 38, 41
NIETZSCHE, F., 108
NO CONSCRIPTION FELLOW-SHIP, the, 12–13
Numbers: existence of, 33, 35–36; reduced by Russell to classes, 36–37, 42; cardinal, defined, 36

OCKHAM's razor, 32
Oligarchy, 140–42
O'NIEL, Colette, *see* MALLESON, Lady Constance
Ontology, 2
Other Minds, problem of one's knowledge of, 101
OXFORD, UNIVERSITY OF, 20

Particulars: and universals, 31–32; whether eliminable, 105, 107–12
Past, status of our belief in the existence of the, 89–90, 101–102
Pastness, feelings of, 90–91
PEANO, Giuseppe, 6
PEARSALL, SMITH, Alys, *see* RUSSELL, Alys
PEARSALL SMITH, Logan, 4
PEIRCE, C. S., 39
Perception: Russell's theories of, 69–86, 100–101; causal theory of, 83, 85
Percepts, 34, 71, 81–82, 85, 87, 100, 104–105, 111, 114–16, 126; standardized, 82, 85
Perspectives, 77–81
Persuasive definitions, 119–20
Philosophy of Bertrand Russell, The, 5, 23, 88
Physical objects: as external causes, 34, 71–76, 82–86, 114; as complexes of qualities, 109–12; as logical

constructions, 77–82, 87–88, 114; perception of, 69, 71–76, 82–83, 109

Physical realism, Russell's, 18, 114–16

Platonic realism, Russell's, 7, 33, 48

Points, 34

Police forces, means of restraining, 150

Political theories, Russell's 138–54

Predicates and subjects, 31, 58

Predicative functions, 46

Prescriptive theory of ethics, 129

Primary data, 34

Primitive propositions of *Principia Mathematica*, 41

Probability: as degree of credibility, 95, 98–99; mathematical, 95–98; of laws, 93–94

Proper names, *see* Names

Propositional functions, 40, 43–44, 46, 51–52, 54, 59; hierarchy of, 45

Propositions: nature of, 40, 62; reality of, 33, 59; affirmative and negative, 65; image and word, 61, 64–67; hierarchy of, 45; and belief, 59–62; and truth, 63–68

Punishment, 122

Qualities: complexes of, 32–33, 58, 76, 108–12; constituting events, 113; constituting physical objects, 109–12; external, 104; simple, 104–105

Quantifiers, 40, 51–53

Quasi-permanence, postulate of, 99–100, 102

QUINE, W. V., 54, 58, 102

RAMSEY, F. P., 56

Realism: naïve, 74–75;

physical, 18, 114–16; scientific, 116

Reality, Russell's conception of, 33–34, 48–49, 55, 103–16

Reducibility, axiom of, 46

Reflection, simple ideas of, 30

Relations: existence of, 31; external, 104; one-one, 36; similarity of, 38

Religious experience, argument from, 132–34

Representative government, 143–44

Right actions: Russell's definition of, 118–19, 127; objectively, 118; subjectively, 118

RUSSELL, Agatha, 4

RUSSELL, Alys, 4–5, 9–11

RUSSELL, Bertrand, Arthur William, 3rd Earl; birth of, 2; childhood of, 2–3; education of, 3–4; marriages of, 5, 17, 20, 25; his engagement in politics, 1, 8–9, 11–15, 17, 25–27, 153–54; his relations with Trinity College, Cambridge, 4–5, 9, 14, 22–23; his academic posts, 5, 9, 14, 20–23; denied a post at City College, New York, 20–21; imprisonment of, 15, 26; his visits to Russia and China, 16–17; founds primary school, 19; succeeds to earldom, 19; honored in his old age, 23–24; death of, 27; agnosticism of, 8–9, 131–34; his analysis of belief, 59–64; his theory of causation, 84, 91–92, 107; his disapproval of Christianity, 134–37; his attitude toward Communism, 17–18, 23, 141, 152; his attitude to conscience, 119, 124;

his theory of descriptions, 10, 47, 48–58, 105; his empiricism, 11, 18, 29, 154; his theories of ethics, 117–30; his account of free will, 120–22; his account of good, 118, 126–27; his theory of induction, 92–102; his theory of knowledge, 54, 69–102; his disapproval of linguistic philosophy, 23; his system of logic, 39–40; his reduction of mathematics to logic, 6, 35–39; his analysis of memory, 32, 89–92; his rejection of mental acts, 60, 71, 89; his rejection of naïve realism, 74–75; his theory of names, 50, 53, 57–58, 105; his dislike of nationalism, 150–51; his theories of perception, 69–86, 100–101; his physical realism, 18, 114–16; his platonic realism, 7, 33, 48; his political theories, 138–54; his conception of reality, 33–34, 48–49, 55, 103–16; his definition of right actions, 118–19, 127; his conception of the self, 32–33, 60, 71, 86–87; his conception of space and time, 76–85, 113; his definition of a sign, 62; his distrust of the State, 148–50; his Socialism, 145–49; his theories of truth, 59, 63–68; his theory of types, 7, 42–48; his theory of universals and particulars, 30–33, 107–12; his utilitarianism, 127–28, 130; his belief in world government, 25, 151–54; his works: *A Critical Exposition of the Philosophy of Leibniz*, 6; *An Essay on the Foundations of Geometry*, 6; *A History of Western Philosophy*, 22; *An Inquiry into Meaning and Truth*, 22, 58, 61, 67, 74, 105, 108, 112; *An Outline of Philosophy*, 18; *Authority and the Individual*, 24; *Common Sense and Nuclear Warfare*, 25; *Determinism and Physics*, 20; *Education and the Social Order*, 134, 138, 150, 152; *Education: Especially in Early Childhood*, 18, 21; *Freedom and Organization 1814–1914*, 19; *German Social Democracy*, 5; *Has Man a Future?* 25; *Human Knowledge: Its Scope and Limits*, 23, 83, 92–93, 95, 98–101, 108–109; *Human Society in Ethics and Politics*, 24, 117, 122–30; *In Praise of Idleness*, 19; *Introduction to Mathematical Philosophy*, 15, 34, 36, 38, 40, 46, 49, 51; *Logic and Knowledge*, 15, 32, 43, 50, 65, 103, 105–108, 112; *Marriage and Morals*, 18; *My Philosophical Development*, 24, 71, 115–16; *Mysticism and Logic*, 8, 35–36, 77–80; *New Hopes for a Changing World*, 152–53; *Nightmares of Eminent Persons*, 25; *Our Knowledge of the External World*, 11, 34, 77, 79; *Philosophical Essays*, 8, 10, 59–60, 117, 119; *Political Ideals*, 142, 146; *Portraits from Memory*, 12, 24, 115, 137; *Power: A New Social Analysis*, 20, 129, 139–41, 143–44, 150; *Principia Mathematica*, 7–10, 15, 44, 51, 59; *Principles of Social*

Reconstruction, 12, 139, 145, 148, 151, *Religion and Science*, 20, 129, 134–35; *Roads to Freedom*, 12, 147–49; *Satan in the Suburbs*, 25; *Sceptical Essays*, 9, 18; *The A.B.C. of Atoms*, 18; *The A.B.C. of Relativity*, 18; *The Amberley Papers*, 2; *The Analysis of Matter*, 18, 82–83; *The Analysis of Mind*, 15, 32, 60–61, 66–67, 71, 87, 89–92, 114; *The Autobiography of Bertrand Russell*, 2, 6, 7, 11, 13, 15, 17, 21; *The Conquest of Happiness*, 18; *The Principles of Mathematics*, 6, 10, 33, 48; *The Problems of Philosophy*, 11, 30–32, 60, 69–73, 76–77, 86–87, 89, 93–94, 106–107; *The Prospects of Industrial Civilization*, 18; *The Scientific Outlook*, 19; *The Theory and Practice of Bolshevism*, 17; *Unpopular Essays*, 144; *War Crimes in Vietnam*, 26; *Which Way to Peace?*, 20; *Why I am not a Christian*, 18, 21, 134–36

RUSSELL, Conrad, 20
RUSSELL, Dora, 16–19
RUSSELL, Edith, 25–26
RUSSELL, Frank, 2nd Earl, 2–3, 19
RUSSELL, John Conrad, 17
RUSSELL, Lord John, 1st Earl Russell, 2, 3
RUSSELL, Lady John, 1st Countess, 2, 3
RUSSELL, Kate, 17
RUSSELL, Patricia, 2, 20, 25

Sampling, fair, need for a postulate of, 97, 99
SANTAYANA, G., 12

SARTRE, Jean-Paul, 26
Satisfaction, as ethical end, 127–29
SCOTT, Sir Walter, 49
Self, the: whether an object of acquaintance, 32, 60, 86–87; whether analyzable in terms of its experiences, 33; a logical fiction, 71
Self-consciousness, 88
Sensation, simple ideas of, 30
Sense-data, 31, 34, 54, 69–71, 76–77, 80, 86–87, 107–108; treated by Russell as private entities, 70–71; Russell's rejection of, 71
Sensibilia, 77, 79, 81–82, 111, 114
SHAW, George Bernard, 8
SHEFFER, H. M., 39
Signs, Russell's definition of, 62
Simple objects, 104
Sin, original, 136
SMITH, *see* PEARSALL SMITH
Social Contract, the, 138–39
Socialism, Russell's, 145–49
SOCRATES, 135
Space: perceptual, 83; perspective, 78–79; physical, 38, 77, 83, 85; private, 76–77, 79–83; unobservable, 84–85; and geometry, 38
Space-time, constitution of, 113
Specious present, the, 92
SPENCE, Patricia, *see* RUSSELL, Patricia
State, the, Russell's distrust of, 148–50
State of nature, 139
STANLEY OF ALDERLEY, 2nd Lord, 2
STOICS, 124
STRAWSON, P. F., 56
Stroke-function, the, 39, 41
Structural postulate, the, 99–102

Subjects and predicates, 31, 58

Substance: concept of, 32, 58; spiritual, 33; and attributes, 58, 108

Syndicalism, 147

Tautologies, 42

Thermodynamics, second law of, 132

Time, Russell's construction of, 79–80

TRINITY COLLEGE, CAMBRIDGE, 4, 5, 9, 14, 18, 22–23

Truth: theories of, 10, 66, 68; Russell's theories of, 59, 63–68

Truth-values, 39, 56, 59, 96

Types, Russell's theory of, 7, 42–48

Uniformity: expectation of, 93; principle of, 95

UNION OF DEMOCRATIC CONTROL, the, 12

Universals: as objects of acquaintance, 30–31; reality of, 30–31, 33, 107; uneliminable, 105–106; and particulars, 31–32

Variables, 40–41, 51–52, 58, 108

Vertical inference, *see* Inference

VICTORIA, Queen, 2

VOLTAIRE, 25

Volumes, classes of, constituting points, 34

WEBB, Beatrice, 8

WEBB, Sidney, 8

WEISS, Paul, 22

WELLS, H. G., 8, 16

WHITEHEAD, Alfred North, 3, 7–9, 12, 39, 41

WHITEHEAD, Mrs. A. N., 8–9

WITTGENSTEIN, Ludwig, 2, 15–16, 29, 42, 65, 112–13

Women, rights of, Russell's campaign for, 9, 154

Word propositions, *see* Propositions

World government, Russell's belief in, 25, 151–54